Embracing the Armor of God

Cris Hoxie

Cris Hoxie
Eph. 6:13

Published by Cris Hoxie, 2023.

EMBRACING THE ARMOR OF GOD

First edition. December 11, 2023.

ISBN: 979-8223037286

Written by Cris Hoxie.

Table of Contents

Prologue....1
FIND STRENGTH IN THE LORD....3
THE STRENGTH OF THE FULL ARMOR....11
RECOGNIZING THE FORCES WE FIGHT....19
THE POWER OF PUTTING ON THE ARMOR....27
SUCCESS IN STANDING FIRM....35
THE BELT OF TRUTH....45
THE BREASTPLATE OF RIGHTEOUSNESS....57
THE GOSPEL OF PEACE....65
THE SHIELD OF FAITH....73
THE HELMET OF SALVATION....83
THE SWORD OF THE SPIRIT....91
PRAYER AND PETITION....101
FIGHT LIKE A SOLDIER....109
Notes....115
ARMOR CONFESSION....119
SALVATION....121
Prayer....123

Dedication

First and foremost, I want to express my heartfelt gratitude to the FA Intercessory group - Pastor Chad Deerman, Betty Gutierrez, and Manuel Soares - for their prayers throughout this project. Without their prayers, I may have lost hope and given up.

A huge thank you goes to my dear friend, Carol Taylor, who diligently acted as my editor from the very beginning of this project and provided constant encouragement. Her support kept me going during moments of discouragement.

I also want to extend my gratitude to Pastor Chad Deerman for his unintentional yet impactful encouragement.

I would like to express my gratitude to a handful of friends - Dena, Eve, and Jackie - for their invaluable assistance in finalizing the wording.

A big thank you goes to Pastor Jim Westheim, for his patience with me during the author picture sessions. As someone who dislikes having their picture taken, his kindness meant a lot.

To my loving husband, Les, I am incredibly grateful for his constant encouragement, smiles, and patience as I talked about this project nonstop.

Thank you to Draft2Digital for their informative emails and educational materials, which provided me with the necessary guidance to successfully navigate the publishing process.

Above all, I want to express my deepest thanks to the Lord, whose promptings led to the creation of this book. If it weren't for His persistent nudges, keeping me awake for several nights in a row, I wouldn't have learned the valuable lesson of simply saying yes to Him. Thank you for choosing me. I love You!

4 I thank my God always for you because of the grace of God which was given you in Christ Jesus. 1 Corinthians 1:4

Prologue

In today's world, we are ravaged with attention-grabbing headlines and news about global events. Wars, abnormal weather patterns, and social unrest dominate our lives. In the face of all this, including our own personal turmoils, how should we react? The goal of Embracing The Armor of God is to strengthen believers in their faith and empower them to stand strong. Every day, as followers of Christ, we are summoned to put on the armor of God - the belt of truth, the breastplate of righteousness, the shoes of the gospel of peace, the shield of faith, and the sword of the Spirit. However, simply having this armor is not enough; we must also understand how to use it effectively. Our ultimate purpose is to gain deep knowledge about each component of this divine armor.

During these difficult times, I extend an invitation to you to explore this resource. It offers valuable assistance in navigating the challenges that impact both our global community and personal lives. Acknowledging that each of us faces unique struggles, this content aims to provide guidance and support on our individual paths.

FIND STRENGTH IN THE LORD

Ephesians 6:10
10 In conclusion, be strong in the Lord [draw your strength from Him and be empowered through your union with Him] and in the power of His [boundless] might.

In this ongoing battle, it is important for each of us to be aware of the war we are in and to actively decide whether or not we will enter into the fight. The world is filled with countless challenges and obstacles, making it essential for us to remain vigilant and prepared when our Commander, Jesus Christ, sounds the alarm. He is the one who leads us and motivates us to take up arms against our ultimate adversary, the devil. This powerful enemy, Satan, constantly roams the earth, seeking opportunities to attack and undermine us in various aspects of our lives. Beware, for he is relentless and cunning, always ready to strike at any moment. Therefore, we must equip ourselves for this spiritual warfare, arming ourselves with the knowledge of God's word and relying on His strength and guidance to overcome the temptations and trials that we may encounter. Let us stand firm in our faith, prepared to confront the challenges that lie ahead, knowing that with Jesus as our Commander, we have the power to overcome any scheme the devil may throw our way.

During the battle in which we find ourselves, we must draw upon the power and strength of the Lord. Our source of strength lies in Jesus, who exemplified this power when God, His Father, resurrected Him from the dead. This extraordinary act of divine intervention demonstrated that Jesus possessed a level of strength beyond human comprehension. As believers, when we are united with Him, we too are fortified by His unmatched power. With this empowerment, we can confidently navigate through the challenges and demands of each day, relying on His strength to sustain us. It is essential to recognize that we are utterly dependent on Him to accomplish anything significant, as our feeble strength is insufficient to stand against the schemes and attacks of the enemy, Satan.

To attain true strength and power, we find ourselves relying on the unwavering strength of Jesus. This strength comes from the inner workings of His Spirit, which provides us with a sign of deep-rooted courage and resilience. However, when it comes to sharing our faith with others, a sense of timidity often overcomes us, preventing us from even uttering the name of Jesus. This apprehension and fear do not originate from God, but rather from the devious schemes of Satan himself. He is cunning and cunningly exploits our vulnerabilities, particularly in our efforts to spread the message of Jesus and all that He has done for us. Satan strives to maintain a veil of secrecy around Jesus, striving to prevent anyone from discovering Him and developing a personal relationship with Him.

King David in the Bible, serves as an excellent example of the complexities of human nature and the enduring power of repentance. Although he was widely regarded as a man after God's own heart, David experienced a moment of weakness when he encountered the stunning beauty of Bathsheba. Understandably, he succumbed to temptation, as any person with a physical desire might. However, what sets David apart is his unwavering commitment to repentance. Even in his darkest moments, he knew that true strength lay in acknowledging his wrongdoings and seeking forgiveness from God. This sincere act of repentance not only restored his relationship with the Almighty but also reinstated him to a righteous standing. David's story serves as a powerful lesson for us all, reminding us that acknowledging our faults and seeking redemption can ultimately lead us back to a place of righteousness and favor in God's eyes.

In the book of 2 Corinthians, the apostle Paul opens up about his weaknesses, acknowledging that like all of us, he too, felt weak at times.[1] But even in these moments of weakness, Paul finds solace and strength in his faith. He understands the power of leaning on the Lord and relying on His strength. It is interesting to consider how someone like Paul, who was so influential and accomplished in his ministry, can be excited about his weaknesses. However, Paul serves as an exemplary figure, demonstrating that true strength is found in recognizing our limitations and surrendering to the strength of the Lord. Through this perspective, we can also embrace our weaknesses and declare that we are strong precisely in our moments of vulnerability. This can only be achieved when we lean onto our faith in Jesus Christ. Sometimes, it may be necessary to exercise patience and hold back from saying or doing something that could potentially harm others, especially our fellow believers. By recognizing and acting on this, we demonstrate the true depth of our strength and the genuine love we have for our brothers and sisters in Christ.

Suffering is not something that anyone would willingly choose, and this includes suffering for our faith in the Lord. However, this is exactly what Jesus has promised us. In the Gospel of John, Jesus Himself states that because the people of the world persecuted Him, they would also persecute us. This is a stark reality that we cannot ignore. It is disheartening to witness the constant persecution that believers face in our world today. Yet, we must remember that we are not to fear the suffering that may come our way. The book of Revelation reassures us that despite the trials we may endure, we are to remain steadfast in our faith, even if it means facing persecution unto death. The level of persecution can vary depending on where one lives, as some countries are known to be more hostile towards Christians than others. However, it is evident that persecution against believers is on the rise, with incidents occurring on a daily basis. Nevertheless, as followers of Christ, we must remain firm in our convictions and trust that God will grant us the strength to endure whatever challenges may come our way.

During times of suffering, it is crucial to remember that we are not alone in our struggles. The presence of Jesus is a constant source of comfort and support, as He is always by our side, guiding us through hardships. Moreover, we are reminded that we are not the only ones facing challenges; in fact, many others are going through similar experiences. This realization brings about a sense of unity and solidarity, as we understand that our suffering is not isolated but rather a shared human experience. Through this awareness, we can find solace in the knowledge that we are not alone in our trials and can lean on one another for support and understanding. In the book of 1 Peter, it encourages us to remember this truth, reminding us not to bear the burden of suffering in isolation, but to find strength and courage in the communion of others facing similar circumstances. Together, we can navigate the difficulties of life, finding comfort and hope in the companionship of Jesus and our fellow human beings.

When we find ourselves facing persecution, it is natural to retreat into our thoughts and emotions, indulging in a pity party of sorts. In these moments, we often feel a profound sense of loneliness, convinced that no one can truly comprehend the pain and struggles we are experiencing. However, it is important to realize that we are not alone in this battle. Others have faced similar hardships and can offer empathy, guidance, and support if we are willing to reach out to them. Additionally, we must remind ourselves of the words spoken to Abraham and Sarah, assert that nothing is too difficult for the Lord.[2] This reminder serves as a source of hope and encouragement, urging us to resist the temptation of succumbing to our persecution and instead press forward with determination and faith.

God's repetition in getting His message across to humanity is a deliberate tactic to capture our attention. He understands that we as human beings learn best through repetitive teaching and reminders. In one instance, He directed His words to a remnant of the Israelites who had survived the Babylonian exile, reminding them that no matter how challenging their circumstances seemed, nothing was too difficult for the Lord. This message was meant to instill hope and confidence in their hearts, reminding them that God was their ultimate source of victory and help.

Moving forward in the Bible, we encounter another powerful affirmation of God's limitless power and ability. In the New Testament, we are again reminded that while certain things may seem impossible for us as mere mortals, with God, all things are possible. This reassurance provides us with a profound understanding that no matter how insurmountable our problems appear, there is always a solution and a path to victory. However, God, in His infinite wisdom and respect for our free will, never imposes Himself on our struggles. He patiently waits for us to invite Him into our lives, expecting us to humble ourselves and seek His help.

These repetitive messages from God serve as a constant reminder that our difficulties and challenges are never too great for Him to handle. He is always ready and willing to guide us toward triumph, but He requires our active participation and invitation. God's repetition not only emphasizes His power but also highlights the importance of our relationship with Him. He lovingly awaits our call and desires to assist us in every aspect of our lives, proving Him to be a gracious and considerate God.

From Luke, there is a powerful reminder of God's limitless power and ability that nothing is too difficult for Him.[3] This message is mentioned multiple times throughout the Bible, emphasizing the importance of understanding and believing in God's infinite capabilities. It is a comforting thought to know that there is nothing in this world that is impossible for Him. God is all-knowing, and He is aware of every problem and obstacle we may face even before we become aware of them ourselves. He knows the challenges we will encounter and understands our emotional responses to them. Therefore, rather than turning to God as a last resort, it is worth considering the idea of seeking His guidance and help as a primary approach. By approaching God first, we can find solace in His unfailing love and wisdom, knowing that He is always ready to assist and guide us through any situation, no matter how impossible it may seem.

When we rely on the strength of the Lord and recognize that our strength comes from Him, we understand the importance of trust. Trusting in God is similar to the unwavering trust we had in our parents as children. We knew that no matter what happened, they would be there to take care of us. If we fell and hurt ourselves, they would immediately come to our aid, cleaning our wounds and putting a bandage on them. Our Heavenly Father operates in the same way. When we stumble or make mistakes, He does not condemn or abandon us like the devil would. Instead, God lovingly lifts us up, allowing us to begin again. This is a process that should occur less frequently as we mature in our faith. With spiritual growth, we gain the wisdom to discern when something is wrong and have the ability to say no to it.

To combat Satan and his schemes, we must rely on the strength that comes from the Lord. However, if we lack trust in God and His strength, our battle against evil will not be successful. Trust is an essential component that complements His strength. When we trust in Him, we experience a shield of faith that assures us that no matter what we face, God will always catch us.[4]

Throughout the Bible, God repeatedly emphasizes the importance of being strong and of good courage. This message is not to be taken lightly, as He consistently urges us to not fear. His repetition of these words implies that we should have no reason to be afraid or weak, for He is constantly by our side. God is our unfailing companion, and we can find great comfort in knowing that He will never leave us alone.

This assurance of His constant presence takes on a whole new level of comfort and security. He has promised that He will never abandon or forsake us. Despite any other responsibilities or matters that may arise, God is never too busy to leave us alone. As we engage in the battles against the forces of evil, we can be certain that God is on our side. He will guide and protect us, offering a helping hand whenever we stumble or fall. We do not face these challenges alone; rather, we face them with the strength and power of God. Our strength pales in comparison to His, so let us cling tightly to Him and rely on His mighty power as we enter into this fight.

THE STRENGTH OF THE FULL ARMOR

Ephesians 6:11
11 Put on the full armor of God [for His precepts are like the splendid armor of a heavily-armed soldier], so that you may be able to [successfully] stand up against all the schemes and the strategies and the deceits of the devil.

In today's modern military, the image of soldiers often portrays them without heavy armor. They typically don helmets, tactical vests, and are armed with guns. However, in ancient times, such as during the era of the Bible, the concept of armor was quite different. Soldiers of that time relied on metal armor for protection. While the details of each piece of armor will be explored in future chapters, it is important to understand that these protective gear served a specific purpose that is relevant to our spiritual armor. As we navigate through our daily lives, we must recognize that our spiritual armor is bestowed upon us by God. Just as the soldiers of Bible days needed their metal armor for protection, we too rely on our spiritual armor, given by God, to shield us from the challenges and temptations we may encounter.

It is crucial for us to always be prepared and put on the whole armor. This means we cannot simply pick and choose which pieces of armor to wear on different days or depending on the situation. We are called to be consistent and diligent in being fully equipped with all aspects of our spiritual armor. Failing to do so can have serious consequences, although these consequences do not come from our Commander in Chief, Jesus. Instead, they originate from our enemy, Satan. Satan is always on the lookout for opportunities to attack and exploit our vulnerabilities. If we have neglected to put on our armor, we have essentially left ourselves defenseless against whatever schemes and attacks he may unleash upon us. Satan closely observes us, identifying the areas in which we are most vulnerable, and he cleverly entices us through temptation. Peter warns us that Satan is prowling around, seeking to devour those who are not adequately protected.[1] Jesus Himself cautioned us about the danger of losing our armor to someone stronger.[2] However, when we are prepared and fortified with the armor of God, Satan's attempts to undermine and strip us of our spiritual protection become futile. With the Lord's strength and relying on His power, we gain the ability to resist and reject Satan's provocations and tactics. By firmly standing our ground and fully embracing the whole armor, we effectively safeguard ourselves against the deceit and destructive devices of our enemy.

In the letter to the Colossians, Paul speaks about the victory of Jesus over Satan. Paul writes about how Jesus disarmed the powers of darkness while He was on the cross.[3] This victory is significant because it showcases the power and authority of Jesus over the enemy. With this in mind, Paul encourages the Colossians, and by extension, all believers, to not rely on their strength and abilities but instead put on the armor of God. By doing so, they acknowledge their dependence on God and His power to overcome the challenges they face in their daily Christian walk. It is a reminder that as children of God, we should not disregard or underestimate the importance of relying on God's strength and guidance. By putting on the armor of God, we intentionally choose to trust in Him and invite Him to be our protector and guide throughout each day.

In the Old Testament, one fascinating aspect is the revelation that God Himself wears armor.[4] This insight challenges our perception that only we, as human beings, need to adorn ourselves with such protection. It reminds us that even the Almighty requires armor. What is particularly inspiring is that through God's example, He shows us precisely how to wear this armor. In imitating God, we strive to emulate the behavior of our earthly fathers here on earth.[5] When it comes to finding the ultimate role model, there is no better example than God Himself.

Paul's message to the Romans echoes this sentiment by emphasizing that we can be more than conquerors.[6] However, achieving such a triumphant state is only possible when we fully embrace and incorporate the entire armor. We cannot afford to leave any part of it behind. In recognizing the significance of wearing the complete armor, we unlock the true potential to transcend adversity and emerge victorious in all aspects of our lives.

The context in which this scripture was written is truly extraordinary. Paul, the author, found himself in a prison, bound to a Roman soldier by chains. It is fascinating to think that in this seemingly bleak situation, Paul had the opportunity to intimately observe each component of the soldier's armor. Rather than succumbing to self-pity and despair over his current circumstances, Paul had a profound encounter with God. Through this divine encounter, Paul was granted a unique insight into the significance of each element of the Christian armor, drawing parallels between the physical armor he observed and the spiritual armor believers are called to equip themselves with. This moment of revelation amidst his adversity showcases Paul's resilience, as he utilized his surroundings as a divine teaching tool. The depth and richness of this scripture is a testament to the powerful way in which God can work even in the most challenging of circumstances.

In our daily lives, we often encounter temptations that lead us astray from goodness and righteousness. These temptations, however, do not manifest themselves in the form of Satan directly appearing before us. Rather, Satan utilizes various means to entice and draw us towards sin. It could be through the influence of individuals who suggest or encourage us to engage in illicit activities, such as a girl flirting with a married man. Additionally, the advancement of technology, particularly the internet, has provided Satan with yet another powerful tool to tempt and deceive us. Yet, amid these trials, we must remember to equip ourselves with spiritual discernment and firmly reject every temptation that comes our way.

When faced with adversities or conflicts caused by certain individuals, it is crucial to bear in mind that they are merely pawns being manipulated by Satan. They often unwittingly become instruments of his manipulation. Realizing this, instead of harboring anger or bitterness towards those individuals, we should direct our efforts toward resisting Satan's influence. By doing so, we can maintain our integrity without causing harm to the unsuspecting person who was used as a vessel in the first place.

Standing is not just a physical act, but an act of spiritual significance as well. It requires us to be anchored in the Word of

God and to rely on His strength rather than our own. As believers, we are called to stand against the forces of darkness and to courageously proclaim our allegiance to the Trinity - God the Father, Jesus Christ, and the Holy Spirit. We cannot afford to leave any aspect of the Trinity out of our standing, for they are not only observing our actions but also waiting eagerly to come to our aid whenever we seek their help.

Standing not only signifies our unwavering faith in God but also reflects our commitment to serve Him faithfully in the face of opposition. It requires resilience, determination, and a firm belief in His promises. Though standing can be challenging at times, we are reassured that with God's armor and strength, we can overcome any obstacles that come our way. So, let us not hesitate to stand and fulfill our calling as faithful followers of Christ, knowing that the entire Trinity is standing with us and empowering us to be victorious in our spiritual battles.

In our journey of faith, we not only face the challenges of the earthly world but also the spiritual battle against Satan and his demons. This battle is undeniably a war that requires us to stand strong and be prepared to fight whenever the occasion demands it. Our adversaries are not mere individuals but the powers of darkness that seek to deceive, tempt, and destroy. They employ every tactic at their disposal, utilizing the influence and ability given to them by the devil himself. We must remain vigilant and ready to confront these spiritual forces, equipped with the armor. Although this battle may not always be visible to the naked eye, its effects are felt in our daily lives and the struggle between good and evil. By acknowledging the reality of this spiritual warfare, we can actively resist and overcome the schemes of the enemy. Together, as believers in Christ, we can unite in prayer and reliance on God's strength, fortified in the knowledge that victory is ultimately ours. Let us persevere and never back down, knowing that our Savior has already conquered the enemy and given us the authority to overcome.

Satan's main strategy is to use people and circumstances to try and lead us astray from our faith. He knows that humans are susceptible to influence, and he will manipulate those around us to tempt us with sinful behaviors or lead us down a destructive path. Whether it's through peer pressure, negative influences, or even loved ones who are struggling in their own faith, Satan will use these individuals as tools to try to weaken our resolve. Additionally, he has the ability to implant thoughts in our minds, though he does not have direct insight into our thoughts. He can subtly contribute ideas or suggestions that go against God's will, tempting us to doubt our beliefs or make choices that are contrary to our spiritual growth. It is crucial for us as Christians to be aware of these tactics and to stay vigilant in our faith, relying on the power of prayer and the guidance of the Holy Spirit to discern and resist the influence of Satan.

Judas' betrayal of Jesus was a significant turning point in the events leading up to the crucifixion. It is believed that Judas' motivation for betraying Jesus was not only greed but also disappointment and disillusionment. Judas may have expected Jesus to establish an earthly kingdom and was disappointed when Jesus revealed that his kingdom was spiritual and not of this world. This disappointment, combined with the influence of Satan, fueled his decision to betray his teacher and friend. After the betrayal, Judas experienced a deep sense of remorse and guilt. He realized the enormity of his actions and the consequences they would have on Jesus' life. Overwhelmed by guilt, he returned the thirty pieces of silver to the religious authorities, acknowledging that he had sinned by betraying innocent blood. However, his remorse was not enough to alleviate his guilt, and the weight of his betrayal proved to be unbearable. Judas' tragic end serves as a cautionary tale of the devastating consequences of betrayal and the destructive power of greed. His suicide is a testament to the immense remorse and despair he felt. However, it is important to note that while Judas played a pivotal role in Jesus' crucifixion, Jesus' ultimate sacrifice was part of a divine plan to bring salvation to humanity. Despite Judas' betrayal, Jesus' love and forgiveness extended even to him.[7]

This may be an extreme example, but it shows how far Satan will go to get done what he wants. In history, there have been instances where individuals who refused to renounce their faith in Christ faced persecution and even death. These acts of martyrdom serve as a testament to the strength of their convictions and the lengths to which evil forces will go to suppress the truth. Sadly, even in present times, we continue to witness a rise in religious persecution across the globe. Christians in certain regions face threats, violence, and even death for simply professing their belief in Christ. This serves as a stark reminder that the battle between good and evil is ongoing, and the enemy will stop at nothing to undermine and eradicate the message of hope and salvation. While standing strong in our faith is essential, the ultimate sacrifice of martyrdom often resonates more powerfully than any spoken words, leaving an indelible impact on those who witness or hear about these acts of unwavering devotion.

Living with our armor on means being prepared for the challenges and obstacles that may come our way. It involves staying grounded in our faith and being conscious of the spiritual battles that surround us. Just like a suit of armor protects soldiers from harm, our spiritual armor equips us to withstand the attacks of the enemy. However, it is important to continuously check and ensure that every piece of our armor is intact. We must be vigilant and not allow complacency or distractions to cause any part of our spiritual protection to weaken or fall off. By remaining alert and strong, we are better equipped to face whatever comes our way. And even though we may encounter challenges and opposition, we can have confidence in the victory that is already ours through Christ. By living in this manner, we can navigate through life's trials with faith, resilience, and the assurance that we are conquerors.

RECOGNIZING THE FORCES WE FIGHT

Ephesians 6:12
12 For our struggle is not against flesh and blood [contending only with physical opponents], but against the rulers, against the powers, against the world forces of this [present] darkness, against the spiritual forces of wickedness in the heavenly (supernatural) places.

To effectively combat Satan, it is crucial to gain a deep understanding of his nature and tactics. To effectively combat Satan, it is crucial to gain a deep understanding of his nature and tactics. Only by unraveling the subtleties of his schemes can we hope to shield ourselves from his influence. As we delve into the depths of his dark realm, we must remain vigilant, for Satan's seductiveness is cunning and his methods are shrouded in deceit. By arming ourselves with knowledge and discernment, we can fortify our defenses and resist his temptations. Satan is a deceptive adversary, renowned for his skillful manipulation and ability to entice individuals towards sinful acts. His power lies in his capacity to exploit our vulnerabilities and weaknesses, cunningly turning them against us. Therefore, it is crucial for us to identify and fortify our own weaknesses, such as pride, greed, or lust, in order to stop

Satan's attempts to gain influence in our lives. Moreover, we must acquaint ourselves with the cunning strategies and tactics he employs, such as deception, doubt, and discouragement.

By discerning these tactics, we can devise effective countermeasures and depend on the unwavering strength and guidance of God to resist his alluring temptations. It is crucial to bear in mind that our ultimate weapon against Satan lies in our unwavering faith and trust in God, coupled with the power of prayer and the diligent study of His Word. By remaining steadfast in our commitment to resist and conquer Satan, we can effectively counteract his influence and earnestly pursue righteousness. Furthermore, it is important to remember that Satan often preys on our weaknesses and vulnerabilities.

Therefore, we must constantly strive to strengthen our spiritual armor through regular fellowship with other believers and seeking guidance from wise mentors. Additionally, cultivating a deep understanding of God's love and grace will enable us to overcome any doubts or fears that Satan may try to instill in our hearts. Ultimately, by relying on God's power and remaining steadfast in our faith, we can confidently face any spiritual battles that come our way.

One of the most significant challenges we must face is the recognition that our struggle is not against other individuals. They are being manipulated by Satan, are merely pawns in his grand scheme. It is crucial that we do not allow ourselves to become entangled with them, as it only serves to hinder our ability to focus effectively. Diverting our attention away from the devil is counterproductive, as it weakens our capacity to concentrate. The devil's power lies in his skill to manipulate people into carrying out his immoral deeds.

To overcome this obstacle, we must adopt a more strategic and professional approach. Instead of engaging in direct confrontation with these people, we should focus on understanding the tactics employed by Satan. By recognizing his methods, we can develop effective countermeasures to protect ourselves and others from falling victim to his manipulation. Furthermore, it is essential to maintain a sense of empathy and compassion towards those who have been deceived by Satan. Rather than viewing them as enemies, we should see them as victims of his influence. This perspective allows us to approach the situation with a level-headed mindset, seeking to guide and support them towards the path of righteousness.

In order to concentrate our efforts on combating the devil's influence, we must remain vigilant and steadfast in our commitment to our values and beliefs. By strengthening our own moral compass, we become less susceptible to his manipulative tactics. Additionally, we should actively educate ourselves and others about the dangers of falling into Satan's grasp, equipping ourselves with the knowledge and tools necessary to resist his temptations.

With unwavering bravery and an indomitable spirit, we stand united in our relentless fight against the forces of darkness and evil. The prevailing presence of these demonic spirits is felt worldwide. It is crucial to acknowledge that Satan's companions are none other than the fallen angels who have fully embraced their demonic nature. As we confront these forces, we must remember that our strength lies not only in our unity but also in our unwavering faith. With each step we take, we defy the darkness and reaffirm our commitment to righteousness. It is through our collective efforts that we can banish these demonic spirits and restore peace and harmony to our world. Let us stand firm in our resolve and continue to shine the light of truth in the face of darkness.

The powers being referred to here extend beyond the supernatural abilities possessed by Satan and his demons. They also encompass the worldly systems and structures that they manipulate and influence. These powers can take on various forms, such as political, economic, and social systems that go against the principles of God. Their ultimate goal is to exert control and authority over individuals, nations, and even the church.

However, as Christians, we have been bestowed with the power and authority by Christ to resist and overcome these powers. By relying on the Holy Spirit and standing firm in our faith, we have the ability to neutralize their influence and render their powers ineffective. It is of utmost importance for believers to acknowledge the reality of this spiritual battle and actively engage in the fight, relying on God's strength and guidance to emerge victorious[1].

As believers, we must remember that this spiritual battle is not fought with physical weapons, but with the armor of God. In this battle, we are not alone; God is with us, and He has equipped us with everything we need to overcome the forces of darkness.

Currently, Satan holds dominion as the ruler of this world. While we acknowledge the temporary nature of this situation, we must still confront and navigate the challenges posed by his demonic forces during this time. Furthermore, it is crucial to understand that God has passed judgment upon Satan and condemned him. However, as believers, we find solace in the knowledge that God's ultimate victory over evil is certain.[2] We must remain steadfast in our faith and trust in His divine plan. In the face of adversity, we are called to resist the temptations of Satan and stand firm in the truth of God's word. Through prayer, worship, and the guidance of the Holy Spirit, we can overcome the challenges presented by the forces of darkness and emerge victorious in the end.

The alarming surge of wickedness in our world is undeniably disheartening, but it is absolutely imperative that we confront and combat it head-on. Since the days of Paradise, Satan has played a significant role in corrupting our world, and his influence only continues to grow. Despite the fact that many may choose to turn a blind eye or deny this harsh reality, we must acknowledge that it is an ongoing battle that we must face each and every day.

To effectively combat this rising evil, it is crucial that we equip ourselves with spiritual armor. Just as physical armor protects a soldier in the midst of combat, our spiritual armor empowers us to stand firm against the cunning schemes and relentless temptations of the enemy. By adorning ourselves with this armor, we become prepared to confront the daunting challenges and temptations that arise in a world increasingly influenced by wickedness.

Our unwavering faith, fervent prayers, and unwavering reliance on God's word serve as the foundation upon which we can triumph over the darkness and make a profound and positive impact on this fallen world. It is through these spiritual practices that we can rise above the chaos and despair, shining a beacon of hope and righteousness amidst the prevailing wickedness.

While the rise of wickedness may be disheartening, we must not give in to despair. Instead, we must confront and combat it with unwavering determination. By equipping ourselves with spiritual armor and relying on our faith, prayers, and God's Word, we can overcome the darkness and become an influence for a positive change in this fallen world.

We are confronted with spiritual forces of wickedness that reside in elevated realms. These realms encompass various levels of heaven, including our very own atmosphere, which can be regarded as a celestial plane. Surrounding us, there exist unseen spiritual entities, both demonic and angelic, which escape our natural perception. However, as our focus lies on the demonic, it is crucial to comprehend the activities occurring in the elevated realms with regards to these demonic forces.

In recent years, there has been an undeniable surge in wickedness and the influence of evil in our society. This can be observed in various aspects, such as the widespread prevalence of immorality, the erosion of traditional values, and the promotion of sinful behaviors. As followers of Christ, it is crucial for us to acknowledge this reality and respond accordingly. Instead of giving in to fear and hiding, we must embrace our role as soldiers of Christ and actively engage in spiritual battle.

We must be fully aware that Satan, the prince of the power of the air, is actively working to deceive and lead unbelievers astray, preventing them from accepting the life-saving knowledge of Jesus. Simultaneously, he relentlessly seeks to tempt and distract believers, striving to turn them away from God. One of his primary tactics is to target the family structure, recognizing that children are particularly vulnerable. However, as believers, we possess the ability to protect our families by surrounding them with a spiritual hedge through prayer. Our prayers hold immense power, especially when we align them with the Word of God. Speaking the Word of God out loud is particularly effective against the schemes of Satan, as he despises the truth contained within it. He is fully aware of what awaits him in the end, but he is determined to delay his demise by any means possible, if not stop it altogether.

Therefore, it is imperative for us to stand firm in our faith, unwavering in the face of evil. We must equip ourselves with the armor of God. By doing so, we can actively combat the forces of darkness and protect ourselves and our loved ones from the clutches of Satan.

In this battle, we must remember that we are not alone. God is with us, and He has promised to never leave nor forsake us.[3] We can find strength and courage in His presence, knowing that He is our ultimate source of protection and victory.

During his three weeks of waiting, Daniel remained unwavering in his faith and continued his fast as a symbol of unwavering dedication to seeking God's guidance. Little did he know that behind the scenes, a fierce battle was unfolding in the spiritual realm. The prince of Persia, who was none other than Satan himself, resisted the angelic being sent to deliver the answer to Daniel's vision.[4] This spiritual conflict serves as a stark reminder that there are unseen forces at play, relentlessly opposing God's plans and purposes for His children.

Despite the delay, Daniel clung to the assurance that God had heard him. This knowledge brings immense comfort to us as well, assuring us that in our moments of waiting and uncertainty, God's heavenly forces are actively engaged in battle, ensuring that His will ultimately triumphs. Therefore, let us find solace and place our trust in the unseen spiritual realm, fully aware that God is tirelessly working on our behalf, even when we are unable to perceive or comprehend the battles being fought on our behalf. As we navigate through the challenges of life, it is essential to remember that our faith in God's plan is not in vain. Just as Daniel held onto his assurance, we too can find strength in knowing that God is always listening and actively working on our behalf. Even when we cannot see the battles being fought, we can trust that His will ultimately triumphs and that He is orchestrating everything for our good.

THE POWER OF PUTTING ON THE ARMOR

Ephesians 6:13

13 Therefore, put on the complete armor of God, so that you will be able to [successfully] resist and stand your ground in the evil day [of danger], and having done everything [that the crisis demands], to stand firm [in your place, fully prepared, immovable, victorious].

Allow the emphasis of the significance of the word "therefore" within this context. When you encounter this powerful term, it serves as a critical cue that demands your attention and prompts you to ponder its purpose. It has been placed here with a specific intention - to encourage you to reflect upon the previous content. By doing so, you are able to gain deeper insights and grasp the underlying connections between ideas, leading to a richer understanding of the message. The content of the previous verses has been to reinforce and emphasize the significance of the armor, but it is crucial to delve deeper and focus on the individual pieces that comprise it. This preliminary discussion has primed us for the moment of actually putting on this powerful armor. By examining each piece in detail, we can fully grasp their roles and understand how they come together to provide protection and strength.

In order to effectively engage in spiritual warfare, it is essential not only to understand the strategies of our opponent but also to have a thorough knowledge of their identity. We have discovered that our adversary in this battle is none other than Satan himself, accompanied by his legion of fallen angels, commonly known as demons. This insight enables us to comprehend the magnitude of the spiritual forces at play and equips us with a deeper understanding of the battle we are called to wage. By recognizing the true nature of these fallen angels who once dwelled in heavenly realms, we gain a clearer perspective on their capabilities and motivations. Armed with this knowledge, we can better prepare ourselves for spiritual combat by donning the armor necessary to withstand their relentless attacks.

When we understand the concept of armor, our thoughts naturally lean towards brave soldiers fearlessly fighting on the battlefield. Just like these valiant warriors, we too are soldiers, but not just any army. We proudly serve in God's mighty army, armed with faith and righteousness as our shield and sword. So let us stand tall and united as soldiers of God's army, ready to face any challenge that comes our way with unwavering conviction and unyielding faith. The spiritual armor provided by God encompasses a multitude of aspects, each crucial for our daily lives. It is imperative that we diligently put on this armor every day, ensuring that we are fully equipped to face any challenges that may arise. By being prepared at all times, regardless of the season or circumstance, we can navigate through life with unwavering strength and resilience. With God's spiritual armor, we can confidently face any situation that comes our way and emerge victorious.

When thinking of a soldier, it is important to understand that they are always fully equipped and prepared for any situation that may arise. Their attire and gear are meticulously designed to provide optimal protection and functionality, regardless of the temperature or personal preferences. Soldiers prioritize their safety above all else, ensuring that they are shielded from potential hazards at all times. Thus, they never compromise their level of coverage based on climate conditions or personal inclinations. In our unpredictable and ever-changing world, the need for being prepared cannot be overstated. Just like a suit of armor, we must ensure that every piece is in place. By equipping ourselves with all the necessary tools and skills, we can confidently face any challenges that may come our way. We never know when a specific part of our armor will be needed, but by having every piece securely fastened, we are ensured that we are always ready to rise to the occasion whenever the time arises.

Not only are we capable of succeeding in standing, but this verse also emphasizes the significance of consistently standing against evil and the challenges it presents. It reminds us that by steadfastly remaining upright, we demonstrate our unwavering commitment to righteousness and our determination to combat any form of malevolence that may arise. In doing so, we exhibit resilience and fortitude in the face of adversity, ensuring that we prevail over darkness and emerge victorious on the day of reckoning.In the current tumultuous times we find ourselves in, it may seem as if we are living in the final days. However, it is important to understand that what may appear as an ominous period can also be viewed as a personal trial. In order to overcome these challenges, we must fortify ourselves and stand strong each day, unwavering against the adversities that Satan will undoubtedly attempt to hurl our way. By cultivating resilience and unwavering determination, we can navigate through these trying times with grace and emerge victorious on the other side.

In the sacred scriptures, specifically in the book of Revelation, the esteemed apostle John bestowed upon the Church of Philadelphia a profound promise.[1] This promise assures us that if we steadfastly persevere in our Christian journey and faithfully adhere to His divine guidance, we shall be spared from enduring the trials and tribulations that await mankind during the terrible end of days. By embracing this promise following in His footsteps, we can find comfort in knowing that our path will be illuminated with hope and deliverance.

In moments of uncertainty and chaos, it is truly a comforting thought to know that what we are experiencing is not the final chapter of our story. We must remember that life has a way of unfolding with unexpected twists and turns, leading us to new beginnings and brighter horizons. This reassurance can give us the strength to persevere through challenging times, knowing that there is always hope on the horizon. So, let us embrace this perspective and find solace in the knowledge that even amidst turmoil, there is a greater purpose waiting for us beyond the current circumstances.

The apostle Paul imparts his wisdom, guiding us to walk carefully in a world filled with evil.[2] It may initially seem as if this teaching contradicts other scriptures, but upon deeper reflection, we find that these seemingly contrasting passages actually harmonize and complement each other. While one passage encourages us to be cautious and vigilant in our actions, the other reminds us that even amidst the presence of evil, we are not to succumb to despair. Instead, it calls us to rise above the darkness and bring forth goodness and light. This apparent contradiction can be seen as a reminder of the complex nature of life itself. We are constantly faced with challenges and temptations that can lead us astray.

However, it is precisely in these moments that we are called upon to exercise discernment and make choices that align with our higher values. By walking carefully in a world where evil exists, we demonstrate our commitment to living a life of integrity and righteousness. We strive to navigate through the treacherous paths while remaining steadfast in our beliefs and principles. Therefore, it is not so much a contradiction as it is a call for balance – an invitation to be aware of the dangers around us while maintaining our faith and purpose. In doing so, we can embody both caution and courage simultaneously – qualities necessary for navigating through this intricate journey called life. Days were very evil when these were written, as it is evil now. But in the end, it will be much worse than it is now. The comfort is that we won't be around for it.

Paul continues here that we need to be wise during this time. This is the time we are living in, as we do see evil around. And as a reminder, we know where this evil comes from. It does not come from God, but from Satan. We need to make the most out of our time that is left on earth. We do not live for ourselves. In today's society, it is easy to become consumed by the idea of self-importance and self-worship. This concept has become increasingly prevalent, as we are constantly bombarded with messages that encourage us to prioritize our own wants and needs above all else. However, it is important to recognize that this mentality can be dangerous and ultimately lead us down a path of emptiness and despair.

Furthermore, deception has become a pervasive issue in our world today. It seems that everywhere we turn, there are individuals or organizations attempting to mislead us for their own gain. As Christians, we must remain vigilant and ensure that we do not allow ourselves to be deceived into believing in anything or anyone besides Jesus Christ.

Therefore, it is crucial that we remain steadfast in our faith and rely on the guidance of God's Word to navigate the challenges of this world. By staying true to our beliefs and prioritizing our relationship with Jesus above all else, we can find peace and fulfillment even amidst the chaos and confusion of modern life.

Standing firm is an essential part of being a faithful believer. It means having an unwavering commitment to God and His Word, as if your feet are cemented to the ground. No matter what obstacles or challenges come your way, you remain steadfast in your faith and continue to follow God's precepts without turning back. You don't run from God or the fight, but instead, you keep moving forward with determination and courage.

Being a child of God is not always easy, as we face daily battles against our enemy. However, we must remind ourselves that this life is temporary and that our ultimate destination is eternity with God. By keeping our focus on Him and trusting in His presence during the fight, we can be confident that we will reach our final destination.

It's important to remember that our choices play a significant role in our walk with God. He allows us the freedom to choose whether or not we will follow Him, even if it means turning away from Him. However, by choosing to stand firm in our faith and rely on His strength, we can overcome any temptation or trial that comes our way.

Throughout history, believers have faced persecution for their faith, just as they do today. That's why it's crucial to put on the full armor of God every day and ensure that no piece falls off or becomes loose. We must remain vigilant in our commitment to Christ and never waver in our devotion to Him.

SUCCESS IN STANDING FIRM

Ephesians 6:14A
14 So stand firm and hold your ground,

As we approach the final part, it serves as a strong reminder of the main points we have previously discussed, emphasizing the great importance of the current message. This crucial moment urges us to explore further the depth of our beliefs, reinforcing the utmost significance of the principles we have already examined. Our standing is not random; instead, it is characterized by unwavering strength and resilience, incorporating the fundamental values that have guided us up to this point. We stand firm, unyielding, firmly rooted in the Word of God, and wholeheartedly devoted to its divine guidance and teachings. Our position is not a passive state, but a deliberate and determined choice to align ourselves with the timeless truths that have been given to us.

As we move forward, we embrace the challenges that come our way, knowing that our unwavering strength and persistence will carry us through. We understand that staying rooted in the Word of God is not just a mere belief, but a way of life that shapes our actions and decisions. With each step we take, we remain committed to upholding the divine guidance and teachings that have been given to us. Our dedication to these timeless truths empowers us to navigate the ever-changing world with grace and purpose.

As we stand steadfast, it is natural to feel the weariness creeping in, tempting us to seek respite in sitting down for a while. However, it is imperative to be mindful of this sensation, for it is precisely at this moment that our adversary, the devil, seeks to exploit our vulnerability. His cunning strategy lies in patiently waiting for our fatigue, seizing the opportunity to unleash his arsenal of temptations and troubles upon us. Yet, we must not give in to his vicious schemes. The key to neutralizing his plans lies in our unwavering resolve and unyielding stance. As we stand strong against his devious tactics, we must remember that our unity is our greatest weapon. Together, we can withstand any storm he throws our way. Our determination to resist his temptations will pave the path to our victory, leaving him powerless in the face of our unwavering spirit.

This scripture emphasizes the importance of being steadfast and immovable, which implies a constant and unwavering dedication. Being steadfast and immovable requires a strong sense of determination and resilience. It means staying committed to our goals and values, even in the face of challenges and obstacles. This scripture reminds us that true success comes from unwavering dedication and the ability to stay focused on our path, no matter what distractions or temptations may arise. By embodying these qualities, we can achieve greatness and make a lasting impact on the world around us.[1] This steadfastness can also be interpreted as being unwavering to the point of exhaustion. When we reach that state of weariness, it becomes tempting to relax, but doing so would be counterproductive.

The message is crystal clear: we must never surrender or relent, for we are working alongside the omnipotent God Almighty. When faced with challenges and obstacles, it is crucial to remember that our steadfastness is not in vain. It is during these moments of exhaustion that our true strength and resilience shine through. By remaining unwavering in our efforts, we demonstrate our unwavering faith in the power of God Almighty. We must trust that He will provide us with the necessary strength and guidance to overcome any adversity that may come our way. So let us continue to persevere, knowing that our unwavering commitment will lead us to victory.

As we strive to emulate Christ, it is crucial to reflect on the fact that He never gave up. He was fully aware of the challenges that awaited Him during His time on earth, yet He willingly endured it all for our sake, with the ultimate goal of securing our eternal salvation. In our pursuit to imitate Him, we find inspiration in His unwavering determination.

When we contemplate the unwavering commitment of Christ, we are reminded of the profound depth of His sacrifice and the insurmountable strength of His resolve. His steadfastness in the face of adversity serves as a compelling example for us to imitate. It is through His unwavering commitment that we discover the stamina to navigate our own trials and tribulations.

While we strive to remain steadfast and persevere, it is crucial to acknowledge that the journey will not be free of obstacles. As we navigate through life's challenges, it is important to remember that obstacles are not meant to discourage us, but rather to test our resilience and faith. These hurdles serve as opportunities for growth and self-discovery, allowing us to develop the necessary skills and character traits to overcome them. By acknowledging the presence of obstacles, we can approach them with a mindset of determination and perseverance, knowing that they are stepping stones towards our ultimate purpose and fulfillment. It is a common misconception that accepting Christ will result in a life of ease.

However, this notion is a deceitful ploy orchestrated by the devil. His aim is to deceive individuals into thinking that they do not need to strengthen themselves with spiritual armor and stand firm against him. The adversary is relentless in his pursuit to trap those who may unknowingly be under his influence. It is crucial for individuals to recognize the cunning tactics employed by the devil and remain vigilant in their spiritual journey. By acknowledging the existence of evil and the need for spiritual armor, one can actively resist the temptations and traps set by the adversary. It is through strengthening oneself with faith, prayer, and righteousness that individuals can stand firm against the devil's influence and protect their souls from his deceitful ploy.

The path of following Christ requires unwavering commitment, as demonstrated by His own resolute dedication. It is a journey that demands persistence and vigilance against the deceptive tactics of the enemy. Remaining faithful to the teachings of Christ necessitates unwavering dedication and perseverance, even in the face of challenges and trials. It is a path that calls for steadfast faith and determination.

One crucial aspect of standing firm lies in our salvation. It is imperative for us to possess unwavering confidence in the security of our salvation. We must be absolutely certain, without a shadow of doubt, that Christ has freed us from the chains of slavery, and we must steadfastly refuse to revert back to that state. This unwavering assurance is emphasized in Galatians, where it declares our freedom from the yoke of slavery.[2]

When we have unwavering confidence in the security of our salvation, we can live our lives with a sense of freedom and purpose. This assurance allows us to fully embrace the abundant life that Christ has promised us. It empowers us to walk boldly in our faith, knowing that we are no longer bound by the chains of sin and condemnation. As we continue to grow in our understanding of this freedom, we are called to share the good news with others, so that they too may experience the joy and liberation that comes from knowing Christ.

In our steadfastness, patience plays a crucial role. In today's fast-paced society, the yearning for immediate satisfaction is widespread. However, in our spiritual journey with God, it is vital to comprehend that His timing operates on a different scale from ours. Consequently, it becomes imperative for us to nurture patience while remaining resolute. It is during these moments of waiting that our faith is tested and strengthened. Instead of becoming discouraged or trying to rush the process, we should embrace the opportunity to grow in patience and trust in God's perfect timing. By remaining resolute in our faith, we can find solace in knowing that God's plans for us are far greater than anything we could ever imagine.[3]

Being resolute entails remaining steadfast, unwavering, and undeterred.[4] Being resolute is a quality that sets individuals apart from the rest. It means staying committed to one's goals and beliefs, even in the face of challenges and obstacles. Resolute individuals possess a strong sense of determination and are willing to put in the necessary effort to achieve their desired outcomes. They understand that setbacks are merely temporary roadblocks and use them as opportunities to learn and grow. This unwavering position is exclusively reserved for the righteous.[5] Only those who uphold moral values and act with integrity can claim this unwavering position. It is a place where honesty and justice prevail, where the righteous find solace and strength.

In a world filled with chaos and uncertainty, this exclusive position serves as a beacon of hope, reminding us of the importance of staying true to God. These individuals have wholeheartedly committed themselves to prayer and deeply engaged with God's Word. As a result, they have experienced a profound spiritual transformation in their lives. Their unwavering dedication to prayer has allowed them to develop a strong connection with God, finding solace and guidance in His presence. By immersing themselves in His Word, they have gained a deeper understanding of His teachings and have been able to apply them to their daily lives. Their commitment to prayer and engagement with God's Word has not only strengthened their faith but has also inspired others to seek a similar level of devotion.

Furthermore, as we engage with God's Word throughout our lives, we come to realize that His plans have been in motion since the very beginning, encompassing not only our individual lives but the entire world. It is a promise that His plans will ultimately come to fruition.[6]

Moreover, as we delve deeper into the teachings of God, we begin to comprehend the grandeur and significance of His divine plan. It becomes evident that His intentions extend far beyond our limited understanding, reaching every corner of existence.

In our journey of faith, we discover that God's plans are not confined to our personal circumstances or fleeting moments of triumph or despair. They transcend the boundaries of time and space, encompassing the past, present, and future. His divine blueprint encompasses the intricate details of our lives, interwoven with the broader narrative of humanity's collective story.

As we immerse ourselves in the wisdom and guidance found within the pages of His Word, we gain a profound appreciation for the magnitude of His plans. We realize that His purposes extend beyond our comprehension, encompassing the intricate complexities of the world we inhabit. It is through this engagement with God's Word that we begin to grasp the depth of His love and the vastness of His vision.

Our journey with God's Word illuminates the truth that His plans have been set in motion since the very beginning. They extend far beyond our individual lives, embracing the entirety of creation. It is a promise that His plans will ultimately come to fruition, bringing about a glorious culmination of His divine purpose.

We can rest assured that His word will not come back to Him void, but rather, it will fulfill His desires and accomplish the purpose for which He sent it.[7] God's word is powerful and unchanging. It holds the promise of bringing about transformation and fulfilling His divine plan. When we trust in His Word, we can have confidence that it will never return empty, but will always produce the intended results. As we meditate on His promises and align our lives with His truth, we can rest assured that His Word will guide us, strengthen us, and lead us into the fulfillment of His purpose for our lives. Therefore, our unwavering trust in God's plans and His faithfulness is essential as we steadfastly hold onto our faith.

To truly comprehend the significance of this, it is crucial to acknowledge the unshakable trust we place in God's divine plans and His unwavering faithfulness. As we stand resolute in our faith, we recognize the sovereign importance of these beliefs.

By placing our complete trust in God's plans and acknowledging His unwavering faithfulness, we fortify our faith and ensure its unwavering strength.

The Bible shows numerous instances where individuals displayed unwavering resolve and steadfastness in their faith. Among these remarkable examples, we find Moses, who fearlessly confronted Pharaoh to secure the release of the Israelites.[8] Furthermore, the Book of Daniel offers us additional examples of unwavering faith. Shadrach, Meshach, and Abednego serve as prime illustrations of their steadfast belief in God's power to rescue them from the fiery furnace. These three men refused to bow down to the golden statue that King Nebuchadnezzar had erected, even when faced with the threat of death. Their unwavering faith in God's ability to deliver them was evident as they confidently declared, "If we are thrown into the blazing furnace, the God we serve is able to deliver us from it."[9] Their trust in God's power and their refusal to compromise their beliefs serve as an inspiration to believers today, reminding us to stand firm in our faith even in the face of adversity.

Similarly, Daniel himself exhibited unwavering faith when he was thrown into the lion's den.[10] Despite the imminent danger, Daniel's faith in God never wavered. As the hungry lions surrounded him, he remained steadfast in his belief that God would protect him. Miraculously, the ferocious beasts did not harm him, showcasing the power of Daniel's faith. This incredible display of unwavering trust serves as a timeless reminder of the strength that faith can provide in the face of adversity.

These accounts serve as powerful reminders of the significance of unwavering trust in God, regardless of the challenges we encounter. The steadfast commitment displayed by these individuals, including notable figures like Peter, John, and even Paul from Jesus' disciples, serves as a profound source of inspiration for all of us. Despite facing adversity and persecution, they remained resolute and unwavering in their faith.

The narratives preserved in the Bible hold immense significance for us, as they serve as cautionary guides on how to navigate through trials and tribulations. These stories offer timeless lessons on the vital importance of standing strong in the face of adversity. In our everyday lives, it is crucial for us to draw strength from these accounts and imitate the unwavering faith displayed by these remarkable individuals. By following their lead, we can discover the courage and determination needed to confront any challenges that may come our way.

It is crucial to acknowledge that rather than backing down in the face of challenging circumstances, we are urged to remain steadfast and resolute. This necessitates a profound conviction and an unwavering belief in the divine blueprint for our lives. By persisting through adversity, we have the potential to emerge even stronger and more resilient than ever before.

THE BELT OF TRUTH

Ephesians 6:14B
So stand firm and hold your ground, having tightened the wide band of truth (personal integrity, moral courage) around your waist.

Without the belt of truth, we are vulnerable to the cunning schemes and manipulations of the enemy. It is through God's Word that we can discern what is right and wrong, what is genuine and counterfeit. The belt of truth enables us to navigate through the murky waters of deception, allowing us to stand firm in our convictions and resist the temptations that surround us.

In a society where truth is often distorted or disregarded altogether, wearing the belt of truth becomes an act of defiance against the prevailing culture. It signifies our commitment to uphold God's standards and live according to His truth, even when it goes against popular opinion.

The belt of truth also reminds us that our faith is not based on mere speculation or personal preferences. It is grounded in an objective reality - the unchanging nature of God's Word. In a world where moral values shift with every passing trend, we can find solace and stability in knowing that God's truth remains constant.

By embracing the belt of truth, we equip ourselves with a powerful tool that allows us to navigate through the murky waters of moral ambiguity. In a society where right and wrong seem to be constantly shifting, this belt becomes our anchor, grounding us on a solid foundation.

In a world dominated by subjective opinions and moral relativism, it is easy to become swayed by popular beliefs or personal biases. But the belt of truth serves as a constant reminder that there is an objective standard beyond our own limited perspectives. It directs us towards God's unchanging truth, which transcends time and cultural norms.

When we put on this belt, we actively choose to reject the lies and deceptions supported by the enemy. We become aware of his cunning tactics designed to distort reality and lead us astray. Armed with discernment, we can identify falsehoods masquerading as truths and avoid falling into their traps.

We understand that truth is not just a concept or a set of facts, but a way of life. It is the foundation upon which we build our relationships, make decisions, and interact with the world around us. When we choose to embrace truth, we are choosing to align ourselves with God's divine nature.

Living in truth means being honest with ourselves and others, even when it's difficult or uncomfortable. It means speaking the truth in love, knowing that our words have the power to heal and restore. It also means being transparent and authentic in our actions, refusing to compromise our values or integrity for personal gain.

In a world filled with deception and half-truths, embracing truth becomes an act of rebellion against the forces that seek to deceive and manipulate. By holding fast to the belt of truth, we become beacons of light in a darkened world, shining God's love and grace into every situation we encounter.

Therefore, just as the belt held the soldier's armor together, truth holds our lives together. It is the core value that guides our decisions and actions, ensuring that we remain steadfast in our faith and commitment to God. Without truth, our integrity crumbles, and our reputation becomes tarnished.

In a world filled with deception and falsehoods, it is essential for us, as Christians, to stand firm in the truth. This means not only speaking the truth but also living it out in every aspect of our lives. Our words should be honest and trustworthy, reflecting the character of Christ who is the manifestation of truth.

When we consistently live in truth, we become a beacon of light in a dark world. Others can look at us and see the authenticity of our faith. Our actions speak louder than words, and when they align with God's truth, they have the power to draw others closer to Him.

Therefore, it is crucial for us to be mindful of our behavior and the impact it has on others. Our actions should align with the teachings of Christ, displaying love, compassion, and forgiveness. When we act in ways that are contrary to these principles, we not only tarnish our own reputation but also misrepresent the character of Christ.

In a world filled with darkness and negativity, our words have the power to bring light and hope. As children of God, we are called to speak truth with grace and kindness. Our words should uplift and encourage others, rather than tearing them down. By choosing what we say carefully, we can demonstrate the transforming power of Christ's love.

Furthermore, our actions and words should reflect consistency and authenticity. It is not enough to simply put on a facade of righteousness; rather, we must strive for genuine transformation from within. This requires humility and self-reflection as we continually seek to align ourselves with Christ's character.

As followers of Christ, we are called to reflect His character and teachings in every aspect of our lives. Our words and actions should align with the truth that Jesus manifests. When we speak of His love, grace, and redemption, it is essential that our lives show these qualities.

Unbelievers often scrutinize Christians, seeking evidence of hypocrisy or insincerity. They long to see if our faith is genuine or merely a facade. It is through our consistent adherence to truth that we can combat their skepticism and demonstrate the authenticity of our beliefs.

Living a life rooted in truth requires us to be honest not only with others but also with ourselves. We must examine our motives, thoughts, and intentions regularly, ensuring they align with the principles taught by Jesus. This self-reflection helps us identify any inconsistencies within us and allows us to make necessary changes.

Moreover, embracing truth means being transparent about our weaknesses and failures. None of us are perfect; we all stumble at times. Jesus Himself declared that He is the truth, affirming His reliability and trustworthiness.[1] By proclaiming Himself as the Truth, Jesus is not only asserting His divine nature but also emphasizing the importance of truth in our lives. He invites us to place our complete trust in Him, knowing that He will never deceive or mislead us. In a world filled with uncertainty and falsehoods, Jesus stands as an unwavering beacon of truth.

When we choose to trust in Jesus, we are not only accepting His teachings but also aligning ourselves with His character. As followers of Christ, we are called to live our lives marked by integrity and honesty. We are encouraged to be truthful in our words, actions, and interactions with others.

Walking in truth means more than just speaking the truth; it encompasses living a life that reflects the values and principles Jesus taught. It means being authentic and genuine in all aspects of our lives – at home, at work, and within our communities. When we walk in truth, we become living testimonies of Christ's love and grace.

However, it is important to remember that worldly behavior is not exclusive to any particular group or religion. Deception and insincerity can be found in individuals from all walks of life, regardless of their religious beliefs. It is crucial not to generalize or stereotype an entire group based on the actions of a few.

Instead of focusing solely on the potential deceitfulness of others, we should prioritize cultivating discernment and wisdom within ourselves. By being vigilant and attentive, we can better navigate through interactions with others, recognizing when someone may not be genuine in their intentions.

Furthermore, it is essential to approach every interaction with love and grace, rather than suspicion or judgment. While some individuals may indeed have ulterior motives, assuming everyone is deceitful can lead to a lack of trust and hinder meaningful connections.

As Christians, our ultimate goal should be to imitate Christ's teachings by spreading love, compassion, and truth in a world filled with uncertainty and division.[2]

This personification of Truth in Jesus Christ holds profound significance. Just as the Word of God is considered absolute and unchanging, so is Jesus' embodiment of Truth. He becomes the living manifestation of divine wisdom, guiding humanity towards understanding and salvation.

When we delve into the scriptures, we encounter various passages that emphasize the connection between Jesus and the Word. In John, not only does it establish Jesus' eternal existence but also equates him with the very essence of God's communication to humanity.

Furthermore, throughout his earthly ministry, Jesus consistently demonstrated a deep understanding and reverence for scripture. He often quoted from the Old Testament, affirming its authority and fulfilling its prophecies through his life and teachings. By doing so, he exemplified how every word spoken or written in accordance with God's will carries immense weight and significance.[3] Also, the Word being inspired by God means that it holds a special significance and authority in the lives of believers. It is not merely a collection of stories or teachings, but rather a divine revelation that provides guidance, wisdom, and understanding.

The inspiration of the Word implies that it's contents were not solely written by human authors but were influenced and guided by the Holy Spirit. This divine influence ensures that the message conveyed in the scriptures is accurate, reliable, and relevant for all generations. Moreover, the inspiration of the Word highlights its timeless nature. Despite being written thousands of years ago, its teachings continue to resonate with people today. The truths contained within its pages are applicable to various aspects of life, including morality, spirituality, relationships, and personal growth.

Furthermore, because the Word is inspired by God, it carries inherent authority. It's teachings are considered absolute and unchanging.[4] What an incredible assurance it is to know that the Bible, composed of various books written by different individuals over centuries, carries the divine imprint of God's truth. The fact that God spoke this Word to each writer, guiding their thoughts and words, gives us a profound sense of comfort and confidence in its authenticity.

In a world filled with uncertainty and constant change, we can find solace in the unchanging nature of God's Word. It stands as a timeless testament to His character, His promises, and His guidance for humanity. The Bible serves as a compass, pointing us towards truth and providing us with wisdom for every aspect of life.

Knowing that God's Word does not return void fills our hearts with hope and encouragement.[5] It means that every word contained within its pages has purpose and power. When we read the Scriptures with an open heart and mind, we can be assured that God will use His Word to transform us from within.

The observation of the temptation of Jesus highlights His incredible wisdom and strength, as well as the power of God's Word. In each encounter with Satan, Jesus consistently relied on Scripture to counter the temptations thrown His way. This response not only showcases Jesus' deep knowledge and understanding of God's Word but also serves as a powerful example for us to follow.

By responding with the Word, Jesus demonstrated that Scripture is not merely a collection of ancient texts but a living and relevant guide for navigating life's challenges. He showed us that God's Word is a powerful weapon against temptation, doubt, and deception. It serves as a source of truth, guidance, and encouragement in our daily lives. Moreover, Jesus' reliance on Scripture reveals His unwavering commitment to obedience and alignment with God's will.[6] Knowing the Word of God is crucial in our journey of faith because it equips us to discern truth from deception. Just as Satan twisted Scripture when tempting Jesus in the wilderness, he continues to distort and manipulate God's Word to deceive and lead us astray.

By studying and meditating on the Word, we gain a deep understanding of its context, teachings, and principles. This knowledge acts as a spiritual armor, guarding our hearts and minds against the enemy's cunning tactics. When faced with temptation or false teachings that seem convincing, we can rely on our familiarity with Scripture to identify any misinterpretations or half-truths.

Moreover, knowing the Word empowers us to respond effectively to challenges and trials. Jesus Himself demonstrated this during His earthly ministry when He countered Satan's temptations with appropriate scriptural responses. By following His example, we learn not only how to resist temptation but also how to live a life that aligns with God's will.

Continuing this train of thought, it is crucial to understand the significance of telling the whole truth, not just in a court of law but in all aspects of life. When we withhold or manipulate information, we are essentially distorting reality and hindering genuine understanding.

In any given situation, there may be a temptation to stop at a point where we feel comfortable, where revealing the complete truth might be inconvenient or uncomfortable. However, by doing so, we are compromising the integrity of our communication and potentially causing harm to ourselves and others.

The concept of telling the whole truth goes beyond mere honesty; it encompasses transparency, accountability, and respect for others' right to know. It is about recognizing that every piece of information contributes to a comprehensive understanding of a situation or an individual's perspective.

In a court of law, witnesses take an oath to tell the whole truth because justice depends on it. Transparency, accountability, and respect for others' right to know are not only crucial in a court of law but also in our everyday lives. Our integrity and reputations as Christians are built upon the foundation of truth. As followers of Christ, we are called to live lives that reflect His teachings and embody His character. This includes being honest, transparent, and accountable in all aspects of our lives.

When we deviate from the truth, whether it be through dishonesty, deceit, or hypocrisy, we not only compromise our own integrity but also tarnish the Christian name. Our actions have the potential to cast doubt on the credibility of our faith and hinder others from experiencing the transforming power of Christ's love.

As Christians, we are entrusted with a responsibility to be ambassadors of truth in a world that often values deception and manipulation. Our commitment to truth should extend beyond just our words but also permeate our thoughts, actions, and interactions with others. By consistently upholding the truth in both big and small matters, we demonstrate our faithfulness to God's commandments and demonstrate the genuine love that Christ taught us.

When we acknowledge that even the smallest lie is a departure from truth, we recognize the importance of integrity in our lives. Honesty should be our guiding principle, for it reflects our character and builds trust with others. However, being human means we are prone to making mistakes and succumbing to temptation.

In those moments when we do slip and tell a white lie, it is crucial not to let guilt consume us. Instead of allowing Satan to condemn and drag us into despair, we must turn to God with a repentant heart. God's love is boundless, and His forgiveness knows no limits.[7] He eagerly waits for us to come before Him, ready to extend His mercy and grace.

Repentance involves more than just asking for forgiveness; it requires a genuine change of heart and a commitment to strive for truthfulness in all aspects of our lives. It is an opportunity for growth and transformation as we learn from our mistakes and seek God's guidance in aligning ourselves with His truth.

When we choose to deviate from the path of truth and disregard God's commandments, we essentially remove or neglect the belt of truth which should be firmly fastened around us. This belt serves as a symbol of our commitment to honesty, integrity, and righteousness.

By consciously choosing dishonesty or deception, we distance ourselves from God's truth and align ourselves with falsehood. In doing so, we become adversaries to His divine purpose and teachings.

When we are not aligned with God's truth, our actions and words may be driven by selfish motives or personal gain rather than by love, compassion, and justice. We may find ourselves compromising our values and principles for temporary benefits or worldly desires.

The statement by Jesus that if we are not with Him we are against Him carries significant implications for our relationship with Him[8]. It suggests that there is no middle ground when it comes to our allegiance to Jesus. We cannot simply be indifferent or passive observers; we are either actively aligned with Him or opposed to Him. By stating that if we aren't with Him, we are against Him, Jesus emphasizes the importance of making a conscious choice regarding our faith and commitment. He calls us to actively choose to follow Him, to surrender our lives to His teachings, and to align ourselves with His values and principles.

This statement challenges us to examine the depth of our relationship with Jesus. Are we truly walking alongside Him, seeking His guidance and living in accordance with His teachings? Or are we merely going through the motions, claiming to be followers while not fully committing ourselves? By acknowledging the truth of Jesus' words and actions, we can gain valuable insights into how we should live our lives. Jesus taught us to love one another unconditionally, to show compassion and forgiveness, and to prioritize the well-being of others above our own desires.

In a world that often promotes self-centeredness and materialism, following Jesus' example can be challenging. However, it is through his teachings that we find guidance on how to navigate the difficulties of life with integrity and purpose.

Jesus' message was not always easy to accept. He challenged societal norms, confronted hypocrisy, and called for personal transformation. Yet, it is precisely in embracing these truths that we can experience true freedom and fulfillment.

When faced with difficult decisions or moral dilemmas, we can turn to Jesus' teachings as a compass for discernment. His words remind us of the importance of honesty, humility, and justice. They encourage us to seek unity amidst diversity and to extend grace even when it seems undeserved.

When we talk about putting on the belt of truth, we are reminded of its significance in a soldier's armor. The belt not only holds everything together but also provides stability and support. Similarly, as followers of Jesus, our foundation is built on the truth that He embodies. As we fasten this belt of truth around us, it serves as a constant reminder to align our lives with His teachings and character.

In a world filled with deception and half-truths, it becomes crucial for us to reflect Jesus' truth in all aspects of our lives. Our words and actions should be guided by His example so that others may see Him through us. Just as Jesus showed love, compassion, forgiveness, and grace to those around Him, we too should imitate these qualities.

THE BREASTPLATE OF RIGHTEOUSNESS

Ephesians 6:14C
. . . having put on the breastplate of righteousness (an upright heart).

During biblical times, Roman soldiers donned a sturdy metal breastplate to safeguard their chests. Similarly, when we examine our own breastplate, we discover that it represents righteousness. Therefore, it is crucial to delve into the true essence of righteousness.

Traditionally, we have been taught that righteousness entails being in a state of harmony with God, and this understanding is indeed accurate. However, righteousness encompasses much more. It involves establishing a profound spiritual connection with God, as believers in Christ are treated as righteous for His sake. Nevertheless, it is disheartening to witness numerous individuals who claim to be Christians but fail to lead a righteous life. As the amplified version of the Bible emphasizes, righteousness stems from having an upright heart. It all originates from within our hearts. We possess the power to either allow God to dwell within us, enabling us to live righteously, or to reject Him. God has bestowed upon us the gift of free will, and He will never impose Himself upon us.

When we choose to invite God into our hearts, we open ourselves up to His guidance and love. By aligning our actions with His teachings, we can lead a life of righteousness and fulfillment. However, if we reject Him, we deny ourselves the opportunity to experience His grace and the blessings that come with it. It is through our free will that we have the power to shape our relationship with God, and it is a responsibility we should approach with humility and reverence.

In the book of Isaiah, we witness the divine act of God adorning Himself with righteousness, as to wearing a protective coat of armor.[1] As God adorns Himself with righteousness, His divine presence becomes a shield against all forms of evil and injustice. This imagery of a protective coat of armor signifies God's unwavering commitment to justice and His willingness to defend His people. Just as a coat of armor provides physical protection, God's righteousness shields us from spiritual harm and guides us towards a path of righteousness.

The concept of God putting on armor may seem unfamiliar to us, but it's not the typical metal armor seen in pictures. Instead, it refers to the armor that encompasses and protects us, much like clothing.

In our terms, righteousness can be likened to a vest that needs to be worn. This analogy becomes clearer when we observe modern-day soldiers wearing bulletproof vests to safeguard their vital organs. Similarly, in our spiritual journey, we must put on our righteousness as a bulletproof vest. This aligns with the previous chapter's discussion on the belt, which serves to secure the vest in its rightful place. In essence, truth acts as the anchor that holds righteousness in position, ensuring it remains where it should be.

As we navigate through life's challenges, it is crucial to remember that our righteousness is not just a mere accessory but a vital protection. Just like a bulletproof vest shields us from harm, our righteousness shields us from the negative influences and temptations of the world. However, it is not enough to simply put on this vest; we must also secure it in place with the belt of truth. The truth acts as an anchor, keeping our righteousness firmly in position and preventing it from being swayed or compromised. By embracing truth and righteousness together, we can ensure that we remain steadfast on our spiritual journey, standing firm in our beliefs and values.

As we proceed further, it becomes evident that the pursuit of righteousness leads to a fulfilling and vibrant life.[2] When we strive to do what is right, not only do we experience a sense of inner peace, but we also inspire those around us. The pursuit of righteousness allows us to make a positive impact on the world and create lasting change. It is through our actions and choices that we can truly live a meaningful and vibrant life. When we choose to act with integrity and uphold moral values, we become beacons of light in a world that often feels dark and uncertain.

Our commitment to doing what is right not only brings us personal fulfillment, but it also serves as a powerful example for others to follow. By consistently making ethical choices, we can contribute to a collective movement towards a more just and compassionate society. Our actions have the potential to create a ripple effect, inspiring others to join us in making a positive difference and leaving a lasting legacy for future generations.

This is not just any kind of life; it is a life of abundance, dedicated to living for Christ.[3] We must always bear in mind that it is Christ who grants us this life. Living a life of abundance dedicated to Christ means constantly seeking His guidance and following His teachings. It is a life filled with love, compassion, and selflessness, as we strive to imitate His example. We must remember that this abundant life is not solely for our own benefit, but also for the growth of others and the spreading of God's message of hope and salvation.

Living a life of abundance dedicated to Christ also means surrendering our own desires and aligning our will with His. It requires us to trust in His plan, even when it may not align with our own understanding. This abundant life is a journey of faith, where we find strength in His presence and find joy in serving others. It is through our actions and words that we can truly reflect His love and bring hope to those around us.

The source of life lies solely in Him; it cannot be obtained from the world. The prevailing mindset of the world suggests that we are trapped in a state of bondage, but in reality, the situation is quite the opposite. The world, under the dominion of Satan, is enslaved to sin.

However, Jesus has liberated us from this enslavement, and we are deeply honored to serve Him for breaking the shackles of sin that once bound us. Through His sacrifice and resurrection, Jesus has not only freed us from the bondage of sin but has also bestowed upon us the gift of eternal life. This newfound freedom empowers us to live a life of purpose and righteousness, guided by His teachings and love. As we embrace this truth, we are called to share the message of salvation with others, offering them the same opportunity to experience the liberating power of Christ's love.

The apostle Paul, in his wisdom, imparted valuable advice to his spiritual son, Timothy, urging him to relentlessly pursue after righteousness.[4] Paul emphasized the importance of living a life of integrity and moral uprightness. He encouraged Timothy to remain steadfast in his pursuit of righteousness, even in the face of challenges and temptations. Paul's words serve as a timeless reminder for all believers to prioritize their spiritual growth and strive to align their actions with God's will.

Imagine Paul speaking directly to us, urging us to relentlessly chase after righteousness and cling to it with unwavering determination. Our pursuit of righteousness is intricately tied to our pursuit of God, for He is the very embodiment of righteousness itself. Paul reminds us that righteousness is not a one-time achievement, but rather a lifelong journey. It requires constant effort and a deep commitment to aligning our thoughts, words, and actions with God's will. As we strive for righteousness, we must also remember that it is not something we can attain on our own strength. We need to rely on God's grace and guidance to lead us on the path of righteousness.

When Jesus delivered the Sermon on the Mount, he imparted a profound message that has come to be known as the Beatitudes.[5] Within this sermon, Jesus emphasized the importance of actively pursuing righteousness in our lives. Jesus taught that righteousness is not simply a passive state of being, but rather an active pursuit. He encouraged his followers to actively seek justice, mercy, and humility in their daily lives.

By emphasizing the importance of actively pursuing righteousness, Jesus challenged his listeners to go beyond mere words and to live out their faith through their actions. He reminded them that true righteousness is not found in empty rituals or religious practices, but in the genuine love and compassion they show towards others. When we do, our needs will be met. He knows what we need and when we need it.

Sometimes, it can be challenging to wait for the fulfillment of our needs, but it is during these moments that we should actively pursue righteousness. By seeking it, we draw closer to God the Father and develop a more intimate relationship with Him. As we actively pursue righteousness, we begin to align our desires with God's will. We learn to trust in His perfect timing and have faith that He will provide for us in His own way. This process of waiting and seeking righteousness not only strengthens our relationship with God but also helps us grow in patience and perseverance. Ultimately, it is through this journey that we discover the true fulfillment and blessings that come from being in sync with God's plan for our lives.

In another scriptural passage, it is revealed that the Lord's eyes are upon the righteous.[6] It is said that the Lord's watchful gaze never wavers, constantly observing the actions and intentions of those who walk the path of righteousness. This divine attention serves as a source of comfort and guidance for the righteous, knowing that their every step is seen and acknowledged by the Almighty. The passage reminds us that the Lord's eyes are not only upon the righteous in times of triumph but also during moments of struggle and adversity, offering comfort and strength in the face of challenges. It is a testament to the unwavering love and care that the Lord lavishes upon those who strive to live a righteous life. He listens to our pleas for help and is prepared to provide aid.

We must acknowledge that the initial plea for help occurred when we asked for the forgiveness of our sins. In that moment, He was present and granted us forgiveness. If He was capable of doing so while we were still trapped in our sinful state, then He undoubtedly possesses the ability to assist His children. This parallels the behavior of our earthly fathers. Whenever we require assistance, they are always prepared to lend a helping hand. If our earthly fathers are willing to do so, then certainly our Heavenly Father will as well. Our Heavenly Father's love and care for us goes beyond what we can comprehend. Just as our earthly fathers are always there to support us, our Heavenly Father is even more eager to guide us through life's challenges. His wisdom and strength are boundless, and He is always ready to extend His hand of grace and mercy. We can find comfort in knowing that we are never alone, for our Heavenly Father is always by our side, ready to provide the help we need.

When contemplating our salvation, it is crucial to acknowledge the immense price paid by Jesus on our behalf. He selflessly sacrificed His own life to grant us eternal life and give to us His righteousness. Prior to this crucial moment, Jesus was entirely free from sin. However, He willingly took upon Himself the sins of the world, giving us freedom.

Therefore, it is solely through Christ that we are able to put on this righteousness. By taking on our sins, He enabled us to stand blameless before the Father. Having gratefully accepted this invaluable gift, we now find ourselves in a state of righteousness, in perfect alignment with God. It is now our responsibility to proudly wear this righteousness as a vest, honoring God.

Consider the significance of the chest, where our heart resides. Our spiritual heart should now be wholly devoted to God, prompting us to eagerly serve Him while wearing in the breastplate of righteousness. As we embrace the righteousness given to us, we must remember that it is not just a symbol to be worn, but a way of life to be lived. Just as a vest protects and covers our physical body, righteousness shields our spiritual being from the temptations and evils of the world. It is through our unwavering commitment to God and His teachings that we can confidently face any challenges that may come our way, knowing that we are protected by the breastplate of righteousness.

THE GOSPEL OF PEACE

Ephesians 6:15
15 and having strapped on your feet the gospel of peace in preparation [to face the enemy with firm-footed stability and the readiness produced by the good news].

In today's world, the concept of peace feels as distant as an unfamiliar land. Turmoil and unrest surround us wherever we turn. As Christians, it may seem unattainable to embrace this peace. However, we must remember that with God, what appears impossible can become possible.[1]

Turmoil and unrest pervade every corner of our existence. Regardless of where we direct our attention, these disturbances persist. Consequently, as followers of Christ, we may find it daunting to experience true peace. Nevertheless, we must not lose sight of the fact that with God, even the most invincible challenges can be overcome. Despite the persistent disturbances that surround us, it is crucial for us, as followers of Christ, to remember that true peace can still be attained. While it may seem discouraging at times, we must hold onto the belief that with God by our side, no challenge is unobtainable. By staying focused on our faith and trusting in His guidance, we can overcome even the most invincible obstacles that come our way.

The Gospel of Peace is truly a remarkable concept that holds immense potential once we grasp the art of embracing it. The term "walking" describes the essence of this concept, as it symbolizes the shoes of our armor that we must put on. This Gospel, known as the Gospel of Christ, serves as the incorporation of peace itself. Once we wear these shoes, a profound sense of confidence envelops us, empowering us to venture forth and share the Gospel with those who have yet to encounter Christ.

It is crucial to acknowledge the adversary who opposes our mission - none other than Satan himself. He ceaselessly endeavors to stop our progress, employing his legions of demons to put up barriers that prevent us from rescuing his people from his clutches. Despite the relentless efforts of Satan, we must remain steadfast in our faith and trust in God's power. With each step we take in these shoes, we are equipped with the armor of God, ready to face any obstacle that comes our way. Our unwavering determination to spread the Gospel will not be deterred by the enemy's tactics, for we know that the light of Christ will always prevail over darkness. As we walk in these shoes, we become beacons of hope, shining God's love and grace into the lives of those who are lost and in need of salvation.

In order to effectively spread the message of peace in a world that seems devoid of it, it is crucial for us to understand the true essence of peace and its divine source. Regrettably, Satan has succeeded in dismantling peace from our world, tempting us to surrender and take no action. However, giving in to this temptation would mean neglecting a vital aspect of our spiritual armor. We must equip ourselves and be prepared to venture forth, sharing the teachings of Jesus. By spreading the teachings of Jesus, we can counteract the influence of Satan and restore peace to our world.

It is our duty to stand strong in our faith and actively resist the temptation to remain passive. Through our actions and words, we can inspire others to join us in the fight against evil and work towards a harmonious and loving society. Let us not be discouraged by the challenges we face, but rather let them fuel our determination to bring about positive change.

In order to attain peace, we are aware that it is bestowed upon us by the Lord.[2] Therefore, it is our duty to seek the Lord's guidance and follow His teachings to maintain and nurture this precious gift of peace. By practicing love, compassion, and forgiveness, we can create a harmonious environment where peace can flourish.

It is essential to remember that peace is not merely the absence of conflict, but a state of inner tranquility that radiates outward, positively impacting our relationships, communities, and the world at large. He does not grant us this peace for the sole purpose of keeping it to ourselves; rather, He bestows it upon us so that we may share it with others.

In light of the current state of the world, plagued by turmoil and the persecution of Christians, it is unnecessary for us to fret over such matters. Our primary focus should be on carrying out His will. As followers of Christ, we are called to be beacons of hope and love in a world filled with darkness. Instead of being consumed by fear and worry, let us trust in His divine plan and purpose for our lives. By staying steadfast in our faith and actively spreading His message of salvation, we can bring light to those who are lost and offer comfort to those who are suffering.

As we embrace the concept of peace, we gradually develop a profound trust in God throughout our journey.[3] His peace is flawless, especially when we consistently focus our thoughts on Him. As we continue to trust in God and focus our thoughts on Him, we begin to experience a sense of calmness in our lives. This peace that comes from God is not dependent on external circumstances but is rooted in our unwavering faith in Him. It becomes a guiding force that helps us navigate through the challenges and uncertainties of life, providing us with strength and assurance. When we observe the world and start to feel anxious, our faith and devotion to Christ can easily transform into fear, leading us to focus on the realm of the devil. It is crucial for us to consistently turn to Christ, regardless of the circumstances. We must exercise caution in our choices of what we watch and listen to, as fear and worry can infiltrate our minds through various sources.

By immersing ourselves in the teachings of Christ and surrounding ourselves with positive influences, we can combat the negative forces that try to infiltrate our minds. It is important to remember that fear is not from God, but rather a tool used by the devil to distract us from our faith. Instead of succumbing to fear, we should focus on strengthening our relationship with Christ through prayer, scripture, and fellowship with other believers. In doing so, we can find peace and reassurance in the midst of a chaotic world.

In his letter to the Colossians, Paul urged them to allow the peace of God to govern their hearts.[4] Paul emphasized that when the peace of God governs their hearts, they will experience a sense of calmness and harmony in all aspects of their lives. He encouraged them to let go of worries and anxieties, trusting in God's sovereignty and provision. By surrendering to the peace of God, they would find strength and guidance to navigate through challenges and make wise decisions.

Paul reminded them that this peace passes all understanding and is a powerful testimony to the transformation work of Christ in their lives. He is the sole source of comfort that we require as we navigate through our daily lives. By receiving this inner peace from Him, we are then able to extend it to others. His presence brings a sense of tranquility that transcends all worldly troubles. With Him by our side, we find solace in the midst of chaos and strength in times of weakness. As we embrace His love and guidance, we become beacons of light, spreading compassion and understanding to those around us.

There is no need for us to feel anxious about the current state of affairs in the world.[5] Instead, we should focus on finding ways to contribute positively and make a difference. This peace surpasses our comprehension, reaching depths far beyond our understanding, as it originates from God. It is not from this world, as the world itself fails to comprehend or embrace true peace. True peace, born from God, surpasses the limitations of human perception. It's essence is pure and untainted, flowing effortlessly through the hearts of those who seek it. In a world consumed by chaos and conflict, this peace stands as a beacon of hope, inviting all to partake in it's quietness and harmony.

Insomnia affects numerous individuals who find themselves preoccupied with various concerns in their personal lives and the state of the world. However, when peace finally comes, granting us the gift of restful slumber, we can attribute it to the Lord's watchful protection[6]. Insomnia can be a relentless companion, causing sleepless nights and restless minds.

The worries and anxieties that plague us during the day often follow us into the night, making it difficult to find comfort in sleep. But when we do manage to find that peace, it feels like a precious gift given to us by our Heavenly Father. The Lord's watchful protection allows us to surrender our concerns and find rest in the embrace of restful sleep.

One of the causes of insomnia is the feeling of insecurity, apart from medical factors. However, it is crucial to acknowledge that our sense of safety ultimately stems from God, who ensures our protection even amidst chaos and persecution. When we recognize that our sense of safety comes from God, we can find comfort and peace in knowing that we are not alone in our struggles. This understanding allows us to let go of our worries and anxieties, enabling us to sleep better at night. By placing our trust in God's protection, we can overcome the feeling of insecurity that often leads to insomnia.

Paul mentioned that peace is one of the components of the fruit of the Spirit.[7] He emphasized that peace is not just a mere absence of conflict, but a deep sense of tranquility and harmony that comes from a relationship with God. He explained that this peace surpasses all understanding and guards our hearts and minds. Paul encouraged believers to cultivate this fruit of the Spirit, allowing it to guide their actions and interactions with others. We understand that peace, being a fruit of the Spirit of God, is both attainable and available to us. It is a constant presence in our lives when we choose to live for Him rather than conforming to the ways of the world.

While we acknowledge that we are indeed living in this world, we have the power to distance ourselves from its negative influences and refrain from engaging in its harmful activities. By focusing on our relationship with God and seeking His guidance, we can cultivate a sense of inner peace. This peace enables us to navigate through life's challenges with grace and strength. It allows us to approach conflicts and difficulties with a calm and compassionate mindset, seeking resolution rather than adding fuel to the fire.

Paul wrote numerous letters to various churches, emphasizing the importance of peace. It is worth noting that the majority of these writings were composed while he was confined within prison walls. Despite the lack of restfulness in such an environment, Paul possessed an unwavering sense of inner peace, radiating the joy of the Lord. Remarkably, he even managed to lead some of his jailers to embrace the teachings of the Lord through his peaceful interactions with them. Although there may have been moments of discouragement, Paul refused to give into despair. He consistently drew strength from the Lord and relied on God's guidance.

In the midst of these challenging times, it is crucial to remember the power of peace and to equip ourselves with the part of the armor of shoes. By doing so, we can confidently venture out into the world and spread the message of the Gospel, enabling others to learn about Christ and find comfort in Him. Wearing protective footwear is crucial, but it is equally vital to fully embrace the full armor.

THE SHIELD OF FAITH

Ephesians 6:16

16 Above all, lift up the [protective] shield of faith with which you can extinguish all the flaming arrows of the evil one.

Faith is the foundation of our daily lives, permeating every aspect of our existence. It is the unwavering belief in the reliability and trustworthiness of people, systems, and objects around us. For instance, when we sit on a chair, we place our faith in its stability, trusting that it will support our weight without faltering. Similarly, as we board an airplane, we have faith in the expertise and skill of the pilot, relying on their ability to navigate the skies and safely transport us to our desired destination. These instances of faith may seem trivial, but they highlight the implicit trust we place in the world around us. Faith is not limited to physical objects or individuals; it extends to intangible concepts as well. We have faith in the justice system, believing that it will uphold fairness and protect our rights. We have faith in our loved ones, relying on their support and care. Faith is an integral part of our lives, anchoring us and providing a sense of security in an uncertain world.

Faith holds immense significance for Christians, as it plays a pivotal role in their spiritual journey. Without faith, it is impossible to please God[1]. For Christians, faith is not just a belief or a concept, but a deeply personal and transforming experience. It is through faith that Christians find strength, hope, and guidance in their relationship with God. It is the foundation upon which they build their lives and make sense of the world around them. Without faith, the Christian journey would lack purpose and meaning, as it is faith that allows them to trust in God's plan and surrender to His will. He has certain expectations of us. However, it is crucial for us to understand the true essence of faith, as God Himself has kindly explained it to us.

Faith involves firmly believing and eagerly anticipating the fulfillment of something even before it becomes a reality.[2] Having faith requires us to trust in God's plan and have confidence in His promises. It is not merely a passive belief, but an active conviction that drives us to take action and persevere through challenges. By embracing the true essence of faith, we can find strength and hope in the midst of uncertainty, knowing that God is faithful to His word. Now, we should not anticipate extravagant things that are unnecessary. Instead, we should have faith that what God has promised in His Word will manifest in our lives.

Just as we had faith for our salvation, we must continue to nurture and strengthen our faith. However, if we neglect to read the Bible personally, we will lack the knowledge and guidance needed to cultivate our faith. Reading the Bible is not just a religious duty, but a source of inspiration and wisdom. It is through the scriptures that we gain a deeper understanding of God's promises and His plan for our lives. By immersing ourselves in His Word, we open ourselves up to the transforming power of His truth. As we meditate on His teachings, our faith is strengthened, and we are equipped to face the challenges that come our way.

In the book of Hebrews, we are presented with a list of individuals whose unwavering faith can serve as a source of inspiration for us.[3] These individuals, such as Abraham, Moses, and Rahab, demonstrated remarkable trust in God despite facing immense challenges and uncertainties. Their stories remind us that faith is not just a mere belief, but a steadfast conviction that propels us to take action and persevere through difficult times. Their unwavering faith serves as a beacon of hope, encouraging us to trust in God's promises and to remain faithful even when the path ahead seems unclear. As we read about their journeys, we are reminded that our own faith can be strengthened and deepened by studying the examples of those who have gone before us. Their stories remind us that we are not alone in our struggles and that God is always faithful to those who put their trust in Him.

Many individuals demonstrate the power of faith, regardless of their background or past actions. It is evident that God can utilize anyone who wholeheartedly believes in Him. Regardless of their past mistakes or shortcomings, individuals who have unwavering faith in God can experience profound transformations. The power of faith knows no boundaries and can touch the lives of people from all walks of life. It is not limited to those who have led virtuous lives or have an unblemished background. In fact, it is often through their struggles and imperfections that individuals find comfort and strength in their faith. God's ability to work through anyone who wholeheartedly believes in Him is a testament to His boundless love and mercy. This serves as a reminder that no one is beyond redemption and that faith has the power to bring about remarkable change in the lives of individuals, regardless of their past actions.

While Paul prayed for the people of Ephesus, his heartfelt plea was for Christ to indwell within them through their unwavering faith.[4] Paul knew that the power of Christ's indwelling presence would transform the lives of the people in Ephesus. He understood that their unwavering faith would serve as a conduit for divine grace and blessings. With every prayer, Paul envisioned a community that would be filled with love, compassion, and a deep understanding of God's truth. He longed for the people to experience the profound peace and joy that comes from having Christ reside within their hearts. His desire was for the Ephesians to embrace this transforming power and allow it to shape their lives, relationships, and every aspect of their being. Understanding this concept may be challenging for our limited human minds, but our unwavering faith enables us to grasp it. The indwelling of Christ within us propels us towards a deeper level of faith. Faith is an indispensable aspect of our existence, as it penetrates every aspect of our lives dedicated to serving Christ.

As we continue to nurture our faith, we begin to realize that it is not just a belief system, but a transforming force that shapes our character and guides our actions. It empowers us to overcome obstacles and face challenges with courage and resilience. Our unwavering faith in Christ's indwelling presence strengthens our resolve to live a life of purpose and meaning. It compels us to extend love, compassion, and forgiveness to others, reflecting the unconditional love that Christ has shown us.

As we live by faith, it is crucial to acknowledge that it entails believing in something that is not yet visible to us.[5] Living by faith requires us to trust in the unseen and have confidence in the unknown. It is a constant reminder that our beliefs and convictions are not solely based on what we can perceive with our senses.

Instead, faith compels us to have a deep-rooted assurance in the existence of something greater than ourselves. It is through faith that we find the strength to persevere in times of uncertainty and the courage to pursue our dreams, even when the path ahead seems unclear.

By embracing faith, we open ourselves up to endless possibilities and allow our lives to be guided by a force that transcends the limitations of our human understanding. Living by faith on a daily basis entails placing our trust in Someone greater than ourselves. It involves embracing faith as our shield, constantly present and protecting us from life's challenges. Living by faith requires us to surrender our fears and doubts, and instead, rely on the power of God. It means acknowledging that we are not alone in our journey and that there is a higher purpose for every obstacle we face.

By embracing faith, we can navigate through the darkest of times with unwavering hope and perseverance. It is through this unwavering trust in God that we find the strength to overcome life's challenges and emerge stronger than ever before. Living by faith is not always easy, but it is a transforming and empowering way to live, allowing us to experience a deeper sense of peace and fulfillment.

Faith serves as a protective shield against the relentless attacks of Satan. It is evident that he hurls fiery arrows or darts in our direction, aiming to lead us astray. These arrows primarily take the form of temptations, designed to make us renounce our devotion to Jesus or tarnish the honorable Christian identity we bear. It is crucial that we remain vigilant and prepared to deflect these arrows. We must not allow ourselves to compromise the reputation associated with being a follower of Christ. Our shield of faith will reject these temptations at every twist and turn, ensuring that we stay firmly on the righteous and narrow path.

As we navigate through life, it is important to remember that our shield of faith not only protects us from the attacks of Satan but also strengthens our relationship with God. By holding onto our faith, we are able to resist the allure of worldly pleasures and stay focused on our spiritual journey. It is through faith that we find the strength to overcome challenges and persevere in times of adversity. Our shield of faith becomes a symbol of our unwavering trust in God's plan for us, allowing us to walk confidently in His light. With each temptation that we deflect, our faith grows stronger, and we become more rooted in our identity as followers of Christ.

When thinking about Satan, we are left reflecting on the nature of the challenges he may present to us. To gain insight into this, it is crucial to understand his character. Primarily, we are aware that he is a liar.[6] When thinking about Satan, we are left reflecting on the nature of the challenges he may present to us. To gain insight into this, it is crucial to understand his character. Primarily, we are aware that he is a liar.

Furthermore, Satan is known for his manipulative tactics and ability to deceive. He preys on our vulnerabilities and exploits them to his advantage. His cunning nature allows him to twist the truth and lead us astray from the path of righteousness. It is important to recognize that Satan's lies often come disguised as enticing temptations, promising immediate gratification but ultimately leading to destruction. Therefore, it is essential to remain vigilant and discerning, constantly seeking the truth and relying on our faith to protect us from his deceitful schemes. In reality, he is the father of lies, indicating his initiation of dishonesty from the very start. He will manipulate facts, which is a deception. His deceitful nature knows no bounds as he weaves intricate webs of falsehoods to serve his own selfish agenda.

With a silver tongue and a cunning mind, he effortlessly distorts the truth, leaving unsuspecting victims in a state of confusion and disbelief. His mastery of manipulation extends beyond mere facts; he expertly plays with emotions, exploiting vulnerabilities and sowing seeds of doubt in the minds of those around him. Like a puppeteer pulling the strings, he orchestrates a symphony of deception, leaving a trail of broken trust and shattered relationships.

Satan, the accuser, will bring forth accusations against us in the presence of God.[7] Satan, the accuser, will bring forth accusations against us in the presence of God. However, we must not be disheartened by Satan's accusations, for we have an advocate in Jesus Christ who intercedes on our behalf.[8]

Despite Satan's relentless attempts to condemn us, God's love and mercy prevail. In God's presence, we find encouragement and reassurance, knowing that our sins have been forgiven through the sacrifice of Jesus. As we stand before God, Satan's accusations hold no power over us, for we are clothed in the righteousness of Christ. Instead of giving in to fear or shame, let us boldly approach the throne of grace, confident in the knowledge that God's grace is greater than any accusation Satan may bring against us.[9] We are fully aware that we stand on the victorious side, as no force can ever triumph over God. Satan, too, acknowledges his position on the losing end.[10] However, his cunning strategy revolves around trying to prevent this ever happening.

Thinking that he can overcome God, he persistently persists in his attempts. Despite Satan's persistent attempts to overcome God, his efforts are in vain. God's power and authority are unmatched, and no force can ever triumph over Him. Satan's cunning strategy may revolve around preventing his defeat, but he fails to realize that his position on the losing end is inevitable. His arrogance blinds him to the fact that God's victory is certain, and his attempts to prevent it only serves to further highlight his own downfall.

In light of recent global events, it is evident that he has escalated his deceitful tactics. He has successfully manipulated our perception, blurring the lines between good and evil, leading us to believe that what is truly wicked is favorable, while what is genuinely honorable is deemed undesirable.[11] As a result, our society has become increasingly divided, with people embracing moral darkness and disregarding the values that once held us together. It is disheartening to witness the breakdown of integrity and the normalization of dishonesty. However, amidst this chaos, it is crucial for us to remain vigilant and discerning. It is imperative that we avoid falling into such a trap. This can be achieved by consistently holding up our shield of faith and placing our unwavering trust in God, regardless of the circumstances we encounter.

By relying on our faith and trust in God, we can navigate through the challenges and temptations that come our way. It is crucial to remember that our faith acts as a shield, protecting us from the negativity and doubts that may try to infiltrate our minds. With unwavering trust in God, we can find strength and courage to face any situation that Satan may put in front of us. This steadfast belief allows us to remain steadfast in our convictions and make decisions that align with God and His Word. As we continue to hold up our shield of faith, we can confidently move forward, knowing that God is guiding our path and providing us with the wisdom and discernment we need.

THE HELMET OF SALVATION

Ephesians 6:17A
17 And take the helmet of salvation.

In today's society, it is quite common to spot individuals wearing various types of head-wear. From baseball caps, which are popular among both men and women, to an abundance of other styles, hats have become a fashion statement. However, amidst this trend, we are called to embrace a different kind of headgear - a helmet. Now, before you conjure up images of the bulky helmets from the past, let me clarify that this is not the case. Instead, we are encouraged to wear our salvation as a helmet, symbolizing its protective and transformative power.

Our salvation serves as a shield, covering our minds and guarding our thoughts. As we navigate through the challenges and temptations that life throws our way, this helmet of salvation becomes our source of wisdom and guidance. It is through our salvation that we find solace and strength, enabling us to stay rooted in our faith and resist the distractions that may lead us astray.

Just as a helmet shields a warrior's head in battle, our salvation acts as a spiritual armor, safeguarding our minds from the assaults of doubt, fear, and temptation. It is a constant reminder of our identity as followers of Christ and the eternal hope that resides within us. By immersing ourselves in the teachings of the Bible, we draw upon the knowledge and truths that our salvation provides, equipping us to face the trials of each day with unwavering faith.

While hats may be a popular accessory in today's world, let us not forget the significance of the helmet of salvation. It serves as a powerful symbol of our commitment to Christ and our desire to live in alignment with His teachings. As we embark on our daily journey, let us put on this helmet, allowing it to shape our thoughts, protect our minds, and guide our actions.

Wearing the helmet of salvation reminds us of the spiritual battle we face each day. Just as a physical helmet shields our head from harm, the helmet of salvation protects our minds from the attacks of the enemy. It serves as a constant reminder to guard our thoughts and filter them through the truth of God's Word. With the helmet securely in place, we can confidently face the challenges and temptations that come our way, knowing that we are equipped with the power of Christ. As we go about our daily lives, let us not only wear the helmet of salvation but also share its significance with others, inviting them to experience the transforming power of a life surrendered to Christ.

Once again, when we examine the book of Isaiah, we encounter a vivid description of God wearing armor.[1] Notably, He adorns His head with salvation, serving as a protective helmet. This conveys a profound message about the divine nature and the significance of salvation in our lives. God's choice to wear armor in Isaiah's description symbolizes His role as our protector and defender. Just as a helmet shields the head, salvation shields us from the dangers and temptations of the world. It reminds us that God is always there to safeguard us and guide us through life's challenges. This concept emphasizes the significance of salvation and motivates us to pursue a profound understanding of it's significance in our lives. Just as we strive to imitate Jesus, who is both God and man, we are called to wear our helmet of salvation in a similar manner.

Our salvation should be worn as a protective helmet, symbolizing it's vital role in safeguarding our spiritual well-being. As we wear our helmet of salvation, we are reminded of the constant need to guard our minds and hearts against the temptations and distractions of the world. This helmet serves as a reminder that our salvation is not just a one-time event, but an ongoing process of renewing our minds and aligning our thoughts with God's truth. By wearing this helmet, we are equipped to face the challenges and battles of life with confidence, knowing that our salvation is secure and our spiritual well-being is protected.

In his letter to the church in Thessalonica, Paul emphasizes the importance of embracing the hope of salvation as a protective helmet.[2] This serves to highlight the significance and impact of this hope in the lives of believers. Paul goes on to explain that this hope of salvation not only protects believers from the attacks of the enemy, but it also gives them a sense of purpose and direction in their lives. He encourages the Thessalonians to hold onto this hope steadfastly, knowing that it is the anchor for their souls in the midst of life's storms. Furthermore, Paul reminds them that this hope is not just a fleeting wish, but a confident assurance based on the promises of God. It is a hope that enables believers to persevere through trials and tribulations, knowing that their ultimate victory is secured in Christ.

When we talk about hope in the context of wearing salvation as a helmet, it signifies an expectation or a confident assurance.

It implies that we anticipate the protection and assurance that salvation brings. However, it is important to note that this hope can only be realized if one has first received salvation. This journey begins with acknowledging our need for salvation, recognizing our sins, and accepting Jesus Christ as our Savior. It is through this act of faith that we can embark on a transformative journey, experiencing the hope and assurance that salvation brings.

When we explore the idea of salvation, we come to realize that it means Yeshua, also known as Jesus. This understanding helps us comprehend that our salvation originates from the selfless sacrifice made by Jesus on our behalf. However, if we delve even deeper, we discover that salvation encompasses more than just salvation; it includes our deliverance, our help, prosperity, security, and victory. Each of these aspects represents the very essence of what Jesus gave up His life for, so that we can experience life eternal. It is important to note that this prosperity does not solely refer to material wealth, but rather to the abundance we find in our spiritual journey with Christ. One can possess all the riches in the world and still be poor if they lack a relationship with Jesus. The first step towards salvation is accepting Jesus' gift, and once we do so, we can confidently embrace the helmet of salvation.

Once we have accepted Jesus' gift of salvation and embraced the helmet of salvation, our lives are transformed in remarkable ways. The power of salvation extends beyond our earthly existence and reaches into the depths of our souls. It brings us hope in times of despair, strength in moments of weakness, and peace amidst the chaos of life. Salvation is not just a one-time event but a lifelong journey of growing closer to God and becoming more like Christ. As we walk this path, we are continually reminded of the incredible love and grace that Jesus has given us. It is through salvation that we find purpose and meaning in life, knowing that we are part of a greater plan and that our lives have eternal significance. With salvation, we are no longer bound by the chains of sin and death but are set free to live abundantly and joyfully in the presence of our Savior.

As we navigate through our daily lives, we often encounter numerous challenges that test our Christian beliefs. It is crucial for us to remain steadfast in our faith and keep our spiritual armor intact, particularly the helmet of salvation. By donning this helmet, we can find the strength and resilience needed to overcome these obstacles.

Throughout the day, various influences may attempt to sway us from our Christian values. However, it is imperative that we stand firm in our commitment to Christ. Just as a helmet protects our head, safeguarding our thoughts and beliefs, our faith acts as a shield against the doubts and temptations that surround us.

Wearing the helmet of salvation not only serves as a symbol of our devotion to Christ but also empowers us to draw strength from Him. It reminds us of the eternal hope and assurance we have in our Savior, Jesus Christ. By embracing this protective headgear, we can confidently face the challenges that come our way, knowing that we are shielded by His love and grace.

In a world where our beliefs may be questioned or challenged, it is essential to remain rooted in our faith. By keeping our spiritual helmet firmly in place, we demonstrate our unwavering commitment to Christ and inspire others to do the same. Let us embrace the strength and courage that comes from wearing the helmet of salvation, allowing it to guide us through each day with unwavering conviction.

Another thing to be aware of is that Satan attempts to put thoughts in our minds. An illustration of this can be found in the story of Eve in the Garden of Eden, where Satan tempts her by highlighting the appealing appearance and pleasant taste of the forbidden fruit.[3] It is crucial to recognize that Satan's tactics have not changed over time. He still seeks to deceive and manipulate us by planting doubts and tempting thoughts in our minds. Just as he targeted Eve in the Garden of Eden, he continues to exploit our weaknesses and desires, luring us towards actions that may seem enticing but ultimately lead to spiritual downfall. Therefore, it is essential to stay vigilant, relying on our faith and discernment to resist his cunning schemes.

It is unclear whether he communicated with her mentally or verbally, but the temptation was present. She pondered over it, gazed at the enticing fruit, and ultimately gave in to it. As she took a bite of the forbidden fruit, a rush of sensations overwhelmed her. It was as if a veil had been lifted, revealing a world of knowledge and understanding that she had never experienced before. The taste was both sweet and bitter, a perfect reflection of the choices she had made. In that moment, she realized that she had crossed a line, forever altering the course of her life. Regret mingled with curiosity as she wondered what other secrets this newfound power held.

Judas Iscariot, one of the twelve disciples chosen by Jesus, also played a significant role. In the scriptures, it is mentioned that Satan entered into Judas, leading him to betray Jesus to the religious authorities.[4] This betrayal ultimately resulted in Jesus' arrest, trial, and crucifixion. The entrance of Satan into Judas' heart is seen as a tragic event, highlighting the influence of evil forces and the complexity of human nature. This event serves as a poignant reminder of the choices individuals make and the consequences that can follow. Judas' betrayal of Jesus was a complex situation with various factors at play.

Although it is unlikely that Judas was possessed, it is evident that Satan influenced him and exploited his weaknesses. Satan likely planted thoughts of greed, resentment, and self-interest in Judas' mind, gradually leading him down a path of betrayal. Moreover, Judas held the position of the treasurer among the disciples, giving him access to the group's finances.[5] This position of trust and responsibility allowed him to exploit the money for his own gain. By giving in to his greed and dishonesty, Judas unintentionally opened the door for Satan's influence to take hold of him more strongly. Even though Judas may not have been possessed, Satan undoubtedly swayed and manipulated him throughout the entire ordeal of betraying Jesus. It is widely acknowledged that after betraying Jesus, he was overcome with deep regret and ultimately ended his own life by hanging himself.[6]

By examining these examples, we can clearly observe the harmful impact of neglecting the helmet of salvation on our lifestyle choices and the thoughts we entertain. It is crucial to acknowledge that not all thoughts originate from Satan himself. Our own human nature, driven by our fleshly desires, can tempt us to engage in actions that contradict the principles of a true Christian. It is essential to recognize that we are capable of making misguided decisions independently, without solely attributing them to Satan's influence.

However, it is important to remember that Satan does play a significant role in influencing our thoughts and actions. He is constantly seeking to deceive and lead us astray from God's truth. Without the helmet of salvation, we become vulnerable to his cunning tactics and manipulations. Satan knows our weaknesses and will exploit them to his advantage. Therefore, it is crucial for us to not only acknowledge our own human nature but also to be vigilant in protecting our minds with the truth of God's Word. By wearing the helmet of salvation, we can guard ourselves against the lies and temptations of the enemy, enabling us to make wise and godly choices in our daily lives.

As we embark on a new day, let us not forget the significance of putting on our helmet of salvation. It is crucial to remain mindful of its presence throughout the day, especially when faced with challenges, temptations, or decisions that contradict the teachings of the Bible. In such moments, it is essential to take a step back, engage in a moment of quiet prayer, and then confidently express our refusal to partake in those actions.

Occasionally, our workplace may demand that we engage in improper practices or even deceive others to advance their business interests. However, we must remember that such actions are essentially wrong. It is undoubtedly challenging to decline such requests, but perhaps these situations serve as tests, as our colleagues may be aware of our Christian beliefs. It is worth noting that non-believers are observant of how Christians should conduct themselves and may deliberately place obstacles in our path. In these instances, it is crucial to keep our helmet of salvation firmly in place and respond in a manner that aligns with the teachings of Jesus.

By enhancing our understanding of the significance of the helmet of salvation, we can navigate the complexities of daily life with grace and integrity. Let us strive to be a shining example of Christ's teachings, unwavering in our commitment to righteousness.

THE SWORD OF THE SPIRIT

Ephesians 6:17B
17 the sword of the Spirit, which is the Word of God.

We have acquired a sword that differs greatly from the cumbersome, oversized swords depicted in pictures. In contrast, Roman soldiers wielded daggers that were conveniently strapped around their waist. These daggers proved invaluable in close combat situations, allowing the soldiers to swiftly draw and thrust them into their adversaries, potentially inflicting fatal wounds. Furthermore, the compact size of these daggers made them ideal for stealthy operations and quick maneuvers. The Roman soldiers' mastery of these weapons was evident in their ability to execute precise strikes with deadly accuracy. The versatility of the dagger allowed them to be used not only for stabbing but also for slashing and parrying, making them indispensable on the battlefield. With their trusty daggers by their side, the Roman soldiers were able to navigate through tight spaces and engage in close-quarters combat with confidence and agility.

The Word of God serves as our powerful dagger or sword, constituting a crucial component of our armor. Satan harbors an intense hatred towards the Word, despite his familiarity with it. He is well aware that it foretells his ultimate defeat in the war against

God. Nevertheless, he relentlessly endeavors to alter the inevitable course of events. Satan's hatred towards the Word is fueled by his deep-rooted pride and refusal to accept his impending downfall. Despite knowing that his defeat is inevitable, he cunningly schemes and manipulates in a desperate attempt to defy fate. His relentless efforts to alter the course of events reveal his unyielding determination and unwavering commitment to his rebellious cause.

When we employ the power of the Word against Satan and his demons, it acts as a formidable weapon, piercing through their defenses. They retreat in the face of its might. It is as if they diminish in size, shrinking away from its influence. In a sense, it is comparable to throwing poison on them, rendering them weak and desperate to escape its effects swiftly. As the powerful force looms over them, their once confident demeanor crumbles into fear and uncertainty. Their once vibrant colors fade, blending into the background as they desperately seek refuge from its overwhelming presence.

In the opening of his Gospel, the apostle John explicitly identifies Jesus as the Word.[1] In the opening of his Gospel, the apostle John explicitly identifies Jesus as the Word. John goes on to explain that Jesus, as the Word, was with God in the beginning and was God Himself. This profound statement highlights the divine nature of Jesus and emphasizes his role in the creation of the world. By referring to Jesus as the Word, John suggests that Jesus is the ultimate expression of God's thoughts, intentions, and teachings. This concept sets the stage for the rest of John's Gospel, where he explores the significance of Jesus' life, ministry, and teachings in relation to the salvation of humanity.

As we wield the Word of God as a powerful sword, we effectively employ Jesus as our divine weapon. With the Word of God in our hands, we are equipped to face any challenge that comes our way. Just as a sword can cut through the toughest armor, the teachings of Jesus can penetrate the darkest corners of our hearts and minds. By embracing His teachings and living according to His example, we become warriors of love, compassion, and forgiveness. As we walk in His footsteps, we bring light to the world and spread His message of hope and salvation. With Jesus as our sword, we have the power to overcome any obstacle and bring about positive change in our lives and the lives of others.

Furthermore, it is evident that this sword possesses the characteristics of a double-edged sword.[2] One of the main advantages of a double-edged sword is its versatility in combat. With a blade that is sharp on both sides, it allows the wielder to strike from multiple angles, making it harder for opponents to defend against. Additionally, the double-edged sword offers a balanced weight distribution, enabling swift and precise movements. However, it also requires a higher level of skill and control to wield effectively, as the potential for self-inflicted injuries is greater. Overall, the characteristics of a double-edged sword make it a formidable weapon in the hands of a skilled warrior.

The previously mentioned swords posed a significant threat, capable of inflicting severe wounds and even causing death. In contrast, our sword is the powerful Word of God. It possesses an active nature, rather than a passive one, and delves deep into the core of matters, leaving no aspect unaddressed. The Word encompasses a vast array of topics that directly impact our lives. The Word of God not only addresses the surface-level issues we face but also penetrates the depths of our hearts and minds. It has the ability to bring clarity to our confusion, healing to our wounds, and guidance to our paths. With its vast wisdom and divine authority, the Word empowers us to navigate the complexities of life and make choices that align with God's will.

The Word of God is divinely inspired and originates from God Himself.[3] The Word of God, being divinely inspired and originating from God Himself, holds immense power and wisdom. It serves as a guiding light for humanity, offering profound insights into the nature of existence and the purpose of life. Through it's teachings, we can find comfort, guidance, and a deeper connection with God. The Holy Spirit divinely inspired individuals to write the Scriptures, providing us with invaluable examples and guidance on how to lead a godly life.

The Bible was not a mere coincidence; rather, it was a result of God directly instructing these individuals on what to write. The Holy Spirit's divine inspiration of the Scriptures ensures that they are not just ordinary writings, but rather a sacred and timeless message from God Himself. Through the Bible, we gain profound insights into the nature of God, His love for humanity, and His plan for our salvation. It serves as a compass, guiding us through life's challenges and offering us hope, comfort, and wisdom in every situation.

As we encounter the temptations that Satan presents, we possess the powerful tool of God's Word to counter his attacks..[4] As we encounter the temptations that Satan presents, we possess the powerful tool of God's Word to counter his attacks. Just as Jesus employed the Word to resist Satan's temptations during his time in the wilderness, we too can draw strength from it. When we immerse ourselves in God's Word, we gain a deeper understanding of His truth and promises. This knowledge equips us to discern between right and wrong, enabling us to make wise choices when faced with temptation. By meditating on Scripture and allowing it to dwell richly within us, we are fortified against the schemes of the enemy.

In our pursuit to imitate Jesus and live as He did, we possess a powerful tool to combat the pervasive darkness of evil - the Word. By harnessing the Word, we can effectively wield it as a weapon. As followers of Jesus, we are called to not only possess the Word but also to internalize it and let it guide our thoughts, words, and actions. The Word has the power to transform our hearts and minds, enabling us to resist temptation and overcome the forces of darkness.

The Word shall also light up our way, acting as a guiding lighthouse for us to pursue.[5] It provides us with moral and ethical principles, guiding us towards righteousness and compassion. Through its wisdom, we gain clarity and understanding, helping us navigate through the complexities and challenges of life. The Word acts as a road map, showing us the right direction and empowering us to make informed decisions. It offers solace and comfort during times of darkness, offering hope and encouragement when we feel lost or confused. By following the Word, we can lead a purposeful and meaningful life, grounded in love, peace, and harmony.

We do not need to conform to what the world and its ways present to us. Instead, we have the guidance of God and His Word to lead us, showing us the path we should take and the actions we should pursue. By following God's guidance and staying true to His Word, we can navigate through the challenges and temptations of the world. His teachings provide us with a moral compass, helping us make decisions that align with His will. With God as our guide, we can find peace, purpose, and fulfillment, even in the midst of a chaotic world.

In order to effectively combat Satan with the Word, it is crucial for us to be prepared and equipped to strike him down. We cannot afford to waste time searching for the right verses in the heat of the battle; instead, we must be ready at all times in and out of season, regardless of the circumstances.[6] In order to effectively combat Satan with the Word, it is crucial for us to be prepared and equipped to strike him down.

We cannot afford to waste time searching for the right verses in the heat of the battle; instead, we must be ready at all times in and out of season, regardless of the circumstances. One way to be prepared is to regularly study and meditate on the Word of God. By immersing ourselves in Scripture, we gain a deeper understanding of its power and are better equipped to wield it against the enemy. Additionally, cultivating a strong prayer life is essential in our fight against Satan. Through prayer, we can seek guidance, strength, and discernment from God, enabling us to effectively use His Word as a weapon. Lastly, surrounding ourselves with fellow believers who share the same passion for spiritual warfare can provide encouragement and accountability as we strive to combat Satan and his schemes.

In order to achieve this, it is imperative that we engage with the Word of God on a daily basis and internalize its teachings within our hearts.[7] In order to achieve this, it is imperative that we engage with the Word of God on a daily basis and internalize its teachings within our hearts. By immersing ourselves in the Word of God, we can gain a deeper understanding of His will and purpose for our lives. As we internalize its teachings, we are equipped with the wisdom and guidance necessary to navigate the challenges and decisions we face each day. The Word of God serves as a source of comfort, inspiration, and strength, empowering us to live a life that is pleasing to Him and beneficial to others. The deeper our we are in the Word, the more it penetrates our hearts. Simultaneously, as we diligently internalize its teachings, we must be prepared for the relentless onslaught of Satan and his demonic forces. However, armed with the sword of the Spirit, we shall fearlessly conquer these adversaries. As we continue to immerse ourselves in the Word, its profound impact on our hearts becomes even more evident. The teachings we internalize not only strengthen our faith but also equip us to face the constant attacks from Satan and his demonic forces. With the sword of the Spirit in our hands, we can boldly confront and overcome any challenges that come our way.

As we engage in reading and internalizing the Word, it is crucial that we do not disregard its teachings. We must strive to retain its wisdom within our hearts, ensuring its lasting impact on our lives.[8] We must strive to retain its wisdom within our hearts, ensuring its lasting impact on our lives. By actively applying the teachings of the Word in our daily lives, we can experience true transformation. It is not enough to simply read and understand the wisdom; we must also live it out in our actions and decisions.

As we consistently practice what we learn, the Word becomes a guiding light, shaping our character and influencing our interactions with others. If you are not actively engaging with the Word, you are going backward. Remaining unmoving is not an option when it comes to your spiritual journey. You have the power to either progress or fall behind, and the choice is yours. Continuing to seek knowledge and understanding of the Word is essential for personal growth. By actively engaging with scripture and applying its teachings to our lives, we can continue to progress on our spiritual journey.

When we utilize the Word, we sending it as if it were a direct message from God Himself. It possesses the power to fulfill its intended purpose.[9] When we approach the Word with reverence and humility, we open ourselves up to receive divine guidance and wisdom. Its words have the ability to touch our hearts and transform our lives. By studying and reflecting upon its teachings, we can find comfort, inspiration, and a deeper understanding of our purpose in this world. Simultaneously, it may not occur immediately. God operates on a different timetable than we do.

While we may desire instant results, it is possible that He has a purpose for the delay. The true Will of God in such circumstances remains unknown to us, but it is crucial to place our trust in Him and persevere without wavering. When faced with delays or unanswered prayers, it is natural to feel frustrated or discouraged. However, it is important to remember that God's timing is perfect and He knows what is best for us. The delay may be a test of our faith or an opportunity for growth and preparation. Instead of becoming disheartened, let us embrace patience and continue to trust in God's plan, knowing that He will bring about the perfect outcome in His own time.

As we wield this sword, it is crucial that we approach it with humility and caution. Pride can hinder the effectiveness of the Word and prevent it from fulfilling its intended purpose. Moreover, we must be mindful of the impact our words and delivery can have, as they possess the power to inflict harm rather than bring about good. Words have the potential to wound deeply, and our actions serve as a reflection of our true intentions.

While it is essential to act out of love, it is equally important to refrain from engaging in personal conflicts without guidance. Even if someone has caused us pain, most likely through hurtful words, we should resist the temptation to retaliate with equally hurtful language. Instead, let us seek guidance from the Holy Spirit and follow His lead in all our endeavors. By refraining from engaging in personal conflicts without guidance, we can maintain our inner peace and avoid escalating the situation further. It is crucial to remember that responding with love and understanding can have a profound impact on resolving conflicts and fostering healthy relationships. Let us strive to be guided by the Holy Spirit, allowing His wisdom to shape our words and actions, even in the face of adversity.

When confronting the devil and his demons, it is most effective to engage in solitude. Stand confident and strong against him, ensuring that he comprehends the identity of the One you serve and the powerful allies fighting alongside you. Victory shall be on your side. Remember, the devil thrives on chaos and distraction. By retreating to solitude, you can silence the noise and focus on your spiritual battle. In the stillness, seek guidance from God and draw strength from your unwavering faith. With the knowledge that you are not alone in this fight, you can face the devil with unwavering determination and emerge victorious.

PRAYER AND PETITION

Ephesians 6:18
18 With all prayer and petition pray [with specific requests] at all times [on every occasion and in every season] in the Spirit, and with this in view, stay alert with all perseverance and petition [interceding in prayer] for all God's people.

Prayer serves as the cornerstone of our spiritual armor, holding everything together. Without prayer, it is the same as going outside without our clothes on. Just as others pray for us, we too must engage in prayer, creating an unbreakable circle of support and connection. Prayer not only strengthens our connection with God, but it also allows us to find comfort and guidance in times of need. It is through prayer that we can express our deepest desires, seek forgiveness, and find the strength to overcome challenges. By engaging in prayer, we open ourselves up to a world of spiritual growth and enlightenment, fostering a sense of peace and tranquility within our souls.

When we engage in prayer, it is important to remember that we direct our prayers to the Father, not to Jesus. This distinction often becomes blurred, but Jesus Himself instructed us to pray to the Father in His name. It is normal for many of us to conclude our prayers in Jesus' name.[1]

When we engage in prayer, it is important to remember that we direct our prayers to the Father, not to Jesus. This distinction often becomes blurred, but Jesus Himself instructed us to pray to the Father in His name. It is normal for many of us to conclude our prayers in Jesus' name. When we pray to the Father in Jesus' name, we acknowledge the role of Jesus as our mediator and advocate.[2] He is the bridge between us and the Father, interceding on our behalf. By praying in Jesus' name, we express our faith in His power and authority. It is through His sacrifice that we have access to the Father, and by praying in His name, we align ourselves with His will and seek His guidance in our lives.

We are instructed to pray at all times. Although it may initially appear challenging, it is actually quite simple to incorporate prayer into our daily lives. It is not necessary to confine ourselves to a prayer room throughout the entire day. Instead, as we navigate through our daily routines, various situations may arise that warrant a brief prayer. For instance, when someone comes to mind, it is an indication that we should pray for them. In such moments, we can silently offer a small prayer on their behalf.

It is important to remember that God is aware of the specific needs requiring prayer at any given moment, and you may not be the only one called upon to offer these small prayers. When we feel prompted to pray for someone, it is a beautiful reminder of our connections and the power of our combined prayers. By offering a small prayer on their behalf, we contribute to a network of support and love. It is comforting to know that we are not alone in our prayers, as God is always attentive to the needs of others and may be calling upon many hearts to intercede for them.

Petitions in prayer are a powerful way to bring specific needs and requests before God. They differ from general prayers in that they focus on specific and tangible outcomes. For example, someone may pray for a loved one who is struggling to find employment, asking for a specific job opportunity to open up for them. Another person may petition for healing for a friend who is battling a specific illness, asking for complete restoration of their health. These petitions acknowledge the unique circumstances and needs of individuals and seek targeted intervention from God. By being specific in our prayers, we demonstrate our faith and trust that God is able to meet our specific needs and provide precise answers.

In his letter to the church of Philippi, Paul emphasizes the importance of expressing our specific requests to God, regardless of the circumstances. He encourages us to bring everything before Him, seeking His guidance and intervention.[3] In his letter to the church of Philippi, Paul emphasizes the importance of expressing our specific requests to God, regardless of the circumstances. He encourages us to bring everything before Him, seeking His guidance and intervention. Paul reminds us that God is not only interested in our big concerns, but also in the smallest details of our lives. He assures us that no request is too insignificant for Him to handle. By bringing everything before God, we acknowledge our dependence on Him and invite Him to work in every area of our lives. Paul's words serve as a reminder that prayer is not just a religious duty, but a powerful tool that connects us to the Almighty and invites His divine intervention.

There is no challenge too great for God.[4] There is no challenge too great for God. His power knows no bounds, and He is always ready to face any obstacle that comes our way. With unwavering faith, we can trust that God will guide us through the toughest of times. His love and strength are our constant companions, giving us the courage to overcome any challenge that life may throw at us. We acknowledge that God has the ability to accomplish it, yet at times, we question whether He will. This uncertainty ultimately comes from our level of trust in God. It is our responsibility to place our trust in Him, believing that He will respond to our prayers and act according to His own timeline, rather than ours.

However, the most challenging aspect lies in the waiting period. It is during this time that we may need to develop greater patience and learn to endure. During the waiting period, it is important to remember that God's timing is perfect and that He knows what is best for us. It is a time for us to reflect on our own desires and align them with His will. This waiting period can be an opportunity for personal growth and spiritual development, as we learn to surrender control and trust in His plan. It may not always be easy, but by embracing patience and endurance, we can find peace and strength in the midst of uncertainty.

In his writings to his spiritual son Timothy, Paul emphasizes the importance of offering prayers and petitions for all individuals.[5] In his writings to his spiritual son Timothy, Paul emphasizes the importance of offering prayers and petitions for all individuals. Paul encourages Timothy to not only offer prayers and petitions for all individuals, but also to do so with a sincere and compassionate heart. He reminds Timothy that prayer is a powerful tool that can bring about positive change in the lives of others. Paul emphasizes the need for Timothy to intercede on behalf of others, lifting their needs and concerns before God. By offering prayers and petitions for all individuals, Timothy can demonstrate his love and care for others, and contribute to the well-being of the community.

No matter who they are or what they believe, it is crucial that we offer our prayers and make specific requests for others. We can have faith that God understands their needs and will provide for them. Prayer is a powerful tool that allows us to connect with God and express our concerns for those around us. By offering our prayers, we not only show compassion but also acknowledge the importance of supporting one another. It is through these heartfelt requests that we can nurture a sense of unity and hope, knowing that our prayers can make a difference in the lives of others.

Paul also wrote to the church in Colossae, addressing the importance of devotion and focus in their prayer life. He urged them to remain steadfast in prayer, emphasizing the need to be alert and attentive.[6] Paul also wrote to the church in Colossae, addressing the importance of devotion and focus in their prayer life. He urged them to remain steadfast in prayer, emphasizing the need to be alert and attentive. Paul encouraged the believers in Colossae to persevere in their prayer life, reminding them that prayer is not just a mere ritual but a powerful means of communication with God. He emphasized the significance of being watchful and attentive in prayer, as it allows believers to align their hearts and minds with God's will. Paul's words served as a reminder that devotion and focus in prayer are essential for spiritual growth and deepening one's relationship with God.

Paul encouraged the Colossians to do all of these actions with a heart filled with thanks. This same message applies to us as well. We are called to be committed to prayer, remaining vigilant to the events unfolding around us. It is crucial to stay aware of the tactics our adversary, the devil, utilizes against us. By maintaining this state of alertness, our prayers become more focused, enabling us to pray with precision. Subsequently, we express our gratitude, but it is important to offer thanks even before witnessing the fulfillment of our prayers. This act of thanksgiving serves as evidence of our unwavering faith in a God who answers our petitions.

We understand that life is full of uncertainties and hardships, but we choose to embrace the power of resilience and faith. With every setback, we view it as an opportunity for growth and learning. We know that surrendering to the challenges will only hinder our progress and hinder our ability to make a positive impact on the lives of those around us. In our pursuit of God's guidance, we recognize the importance of selflessness and compassion.

We do not limit our focus to our own needs in our petitions, but extend to the critical needs of others who find themselves in desperate situations. We firmly believe that by dedicating ourselves wholeheartedly to seeking God's intervention, we can become instruments of hope, fostering transformative change in the world. By persistently seeking God's intervention, we firmly believe that we can become vehicles of hope, dedicated to bringing about positive change in the world. In addition to that, we want to emphasize that our commitment to addressing the urgent needs of individuals in unfortunate circumstances remains unwavering.

In the midst of our daily routines, it is crucial to remember the most vital component of our spiritual armor - prayer and petition. This powerful practice can be incorporated seamlessly into our lives, whether we are at work, running errands, or engaged in any other activity. It is imperative that we never give in to the temptation of giving up. Let us always bear in mind that we are conquerors, for we stand alongside God and are His beloved children. With this mindset, we can overcome any obstacle that comes our way. Every challenge is an opportunity for growth and learning. By staying committed and persistent, we can achieve greatness and fulfill our true potential. It is important to remember that setbacks and failures are not indicators of our abilities, but rather stepping stones towards success. Embracing a positive attitude allows us to view these obstacles as valuable learning experiences. With determination and persistence, we can transform challenges into opportunities for personal and professional growth.

FIGHT LIKE A SOLDIER

2 Timothy 2:3-4
3 Take with me your share of hardship [passing through the difficulties which you are called to endure], like a good soldier of Christ Jesus. 4 No soldier in active service gets entangled in the [ordinary business] affairs of civilian life; [he avoids them] so that he may please the one who enlisted him to serve.

As we have examined each component of our armor, we equip ourselves to become exceptional soldiers in service of God. It is crucial to bear in mind the significance of putting on each piece of this armor on a daily basis. By understanding the purpose and function of every component, we ensure that we are fully prepared for the battles we may face. Each piece serves as a reminder of our commitment to our faith and our duty to protect and serve. As we put our armor on each day, we strengthen our resolve and fortify our spiritual defenses, ready to face any challenges that may come our way.

The first component is the Belt of Truth, symbolizing our commitment to upholding the esteemed Christian reputation with unwavering integrity. The Belt of Truth serves as a constant reminder of our dedication to living a life of honesty and transparency. It signifies our unwavering belief in the power of truth and our commitment to upholding the highest moral standards. With this symbolic belt, we strive to maintain the esteemed Christian reputation by always speaking the truth, acting with integrity, and standing up for what is right. It is a testament to our unwavering commitment to living a life that aligns with our Christian values.

The breastplate of righteousness, which represents an upright heart, is crucial for us to lead lives that mirror the example set by Christ himself. Living with an upright heart means embracing the values of honesty, integrity, and moral righteousness. Just as the breastplate protects the vital organs, our commitment to righteousness shields us from the temptations and vices that can corrupt our souls. By following Christ's example, we can inspire others to lead lives of virtue and make a positive impact on the world around us.

The significance of the Gospel of peace in our lives is crucial for us to actively seek opportunities to share the message of Jesus as we navigate through our daily routines. By doing so, we establish a firm and unwavering stand against the widespread forces of evil that exist in our world. Furthermore, spreading the Gospel of peace not only helps combat evil, but it also brings hope and healing to those who are lost and broken. Through sharing the message of Jesus, we can offer a sense of purpose and direction to individuals who may be searching for meaning in their lives. By actively engaging in this mission, we become agents of positive change, bringing light into the darkness and inspiring others to follow the path of love and compassion.

Above all, as stated in Ephesians, we must put on the Shield of Faith.[1] Our unwavering belief in God and His limitless power holds immense significance. It serves as a guiding light, aiding us in navigating through the challenges that arise in our daily lives. Our faith persists even in the absence of tangible evidence, steadfastly trusting in the unseen. Our belief in God's power also instills a sense of hope and tenacity within us. It reminds us that no matter how difficult the circumstances may be, there is always a higher purpose and a divine plan at play. Our faith gives us the strength to face adversity with courage and resilience. It teaches us to find comfort in the midst of uncertainty and to persevere through life's challenges.

The helmet of salvation is a crucial piece of spiritual armor that protects our minds and thoughts. It serves as a constant reminder of the incredible sacrifice and love that Christ demonstrated for us on the cross. As we engage in the ongoing battle against spiritual forces of evil, let us not forget the significance of our salvation and the victory that Christ's death and resurrection have already achieved. By putting on the helmet of salvation, we are acknowledging our complete reliance on Him as our Commander, seeking His guidance and strength in the midst of the fight. It reminds us to stand firm in our faith and to guard our minds against doubt, fear, and deception. With the helmet of salvation firmly in place, we can confidently face the challenges and trials that come our way, knowing that the saving grace of Christ protect and empower us.

The Word of God, referred to as the Sword of the Spirit, is a powerful spiritual weapon that enables believers to combat the attacks of Satan. It is not a physical weapon, but rather a metaphorical one, representing the authority and power of God's truth. When we engage with the Word of God, studying and meditating on its teachings, we equip ourselves with a powerful tool to resist the schemes and temptations of the enemy.

Satan despises the Word of God because it exposes his lies and reveals the truth that sets people free. Just as a dagger can swiftly strike and incapacitate an opponent, the Word of God, when spoken and declared with faith, can pierce through darkness, confusion, and deception, bringing light and clarity to our spiritual battles. It's truths have the ability to demolish strongholds, break chains, and bring about a transformation in both our lives and the lives of those we intercede for. Therefore, it is crucial for believers to grasp the significance of the Word of God and wield it effectively, standing firm against the enemy's attacks and advancing the Kingdom of God.

Our final piece is prayer. Unfortunately, many individuals tend to overlook its significance as a crucial component of our armor. However, prayer holds immense importance and should never be underestimated. It is imperative that we remain in a constant state of prayer, regardless of the situation at hand. Prayer should be our primary source of guidance, rather than a last resort. Prayer not only helps us connect with God, but it also allows us to find inner peace and strength. It is through prayer that we can seek clarity and wisdom to navigate through life's challenges. By making prayer a regular part of our lives, we cultivate a deep sense of faith and trust in the divine plan. It is a powerful tool that can provide comfort, and hope, even in the darkest of times.

After putting all the necessary pieces on, we are now prepared to venture forth and confront the enemy. Though our adversary may possess cunning and resourcefulness, we possess an unwavering faith in the Almighty. You may have observed the absence of any protective covering on the back. This deliberate omission symbolizes our trust in God's unwavering support. We can rest assured that He will never forsake us in our endeavors.

Now, let us venture forth and engage in battle! As we step onto the battlefield, our hearts fill with determination and our minds sharpen with focus. The clash of swords and the roar of war cries echo in the air, fueling our adrenaline. With unwavering courage, we charge forward, ready to face any challenge that comes our way. Victory awaits us, and we shall emerge triumphant!

Notes

Chapter 1

2 Corinthians 12:10

Genesis 18:14

Luke 1:37

Psalm 28:7

Chapter 2

1 Peter 5:8

Luke 11:21-22

Colossians 2:15

Isaiah 59:17

Ephesians 5:1

Romans 8:37

Luke 23:34; Matthew 27:5

Chapter 3

James 4:7

John 16:11

Hebrews 13:5

Daniel 10

Chapter 4

Revelation 3:10

Ephesians 5:15-16

Chapter 5

1 Corinthians 15:58
Galatians 5:1
James 5:8
Psalm 112:6
Proverbs 12:3
Psalm 33:11-12
Isaiah 55:11
Exodus 4-11
Daniel 3
Daniel 9

Chapter 6

John 14:6
1 Timothy 4:1-2
John 1:1
2 Timothy 3:16
Isaiah 55:11
Matthew 4:1-9
1 John 1:9
Matthew 12:30

Chapter 7

Isaiah 59:17
Proverbs 21:21
John 10:10
1 Timothy 6:7
Matthew 6:33
Psalm 34:15
2 Corinthians 5:21

Chapter 8

Matthew 19:26

2 Thessalonians 3:16
Isaiah 26:3
Colossians 3:15
Philippians 4:6-7
Psalm 4:8
Galatians 5:22

Chapter 9

Hebrews 11:6
Hebrews 11:1
Hebrews 11
Ephesians 3:16-17
2 Corinthians 5:7
John 8:44
Revelation 12:10
1 John 2:1
Hebrews 4:16
Revelation 20:10
Isaiah 5:20

Chapter 10

Isaiah 59:17
1 Thessalonians 5:8 NKJV
Genesis 3:1-7
John 13:27
John 12:6
Matthew 27:3-5

Chapter 11

John 1:1
Hebrews 4:12
2 Timothy 3:16

Matthew 4:4
Psalm 119:105
2 Timothy 4:2
Psalm 119:11
Luke 11:28
Isaiah 55:11

Chapter 12

John 16:23-24
1 John 2:1
Philippians 4:6 AMP
Jeremiah 32:17,27
1 Timothy 2:1
Colossians 4:2

Chapter 13

Ephesians 6:16

ARMOR CONFESSION

Father, in the name of Jesus, I come before you to confess and prepare myself for battle. Thank you for providing me with the necessary tools to fight against evil forces that may come my way.

I am strong and empowered through my union with Him and in the power of His boundless might. Therefore, I put on the FULL armor of God like a heavily-armed soldier so that I can withstand any attack from the devil throughout this day.

My struggle is not against people but against spiritual wickedness orchestrated by Satan. Although he may use individuals as his pawns, my focus remains on him alone.

With this understanding, I now wear the FULL and COMPLETE armor of God so I can resist successfully and stand firm when faced with adversity. As I stand tall, fully prepared for whatever comes my way, I tighten the Belt of Truth around my waist while donning the Breastplate of Righteousness - an upright heart.

I strap onto my feet The Gospel of Peace ready at all times to share it with anyone whom The Holy Spirit nudges me towards while lifting up above all else - The Shield Of Faith which extinguishes those fiery darts thrown by Satan.

SALVATION

In order to proceed with putting on your armor, there is a single prerequisite that must be completed. In order to fully embrace the teachings and values of our faith, it is necessary for you to have become a child of God. The presence of Him is essential for you to have any chance of reaching Heaven.

Romans 10:9-10

9 because if you acknowledge and confess with your mouth that Jesus is Lord [recognizing His power, authority, and majesty as God], and believe in your heart that God raised Him from the dead, you will be saved. 10 For with the heart a person believes [in Christ as Savior] resulting in his justification [that is, being made righteous—being freed of the guilt of sin and made acceptable to God]; and with the mouth he acknowledges and confesses [his faith openly], resulting in and confirming [his] salvation.

Prayer

I am filled with gratitude and appreciation, Lord God, for the incredible sacrifice of sending Jesus to earth. It is through his selfless act on Calvary that I am saved from the weight of my sins. My earnest plea to you is to grant me forgiveness and remove the stain of my sins. I have faith in the belief that Jesus Christ, the Son of God, willingly sacrificed his life on the cross to redeem humanity from sin. His death was not in vain, as he triumphantly rose from the dead after three days, demonstrating his power over death and offering the promise of eternal life to all who believe in him. Today, I firmly believe that Jesus resides in Heaven, seated at the right hand of God, interceding on behalf of those who trust in him. His resurrection serves as a testament to his divinity and the hope he brings to mankind. I thank you, Jesus, for doing this for me and I accept your salvation. Help me to live the rest of my days for You. Thank you. In Jesus Name, Amen.

Don't miss out!

Visit the website below and you can sign up to receive emails whenever Cris Hoxie publishes a new book. There's no charge and no obligation.

https://books2read.com/r/B-A-PJFBB-VNLRC

BOOKS 2 READ

Connecting independent readers to independent writers.

About the Author

Cris Hoxie has been rooted in northern Michigan For the majority of her life. Furthermore, she has graduated from Ames International School of the Bible and holds a deep passion for reading. Over the course of six years, she has been engaged as a book reviewer while concurrently generating devotionals for eight years for a Facebook community.

Cris's love for snow was instilled in her by her Northern Michigan upbringing. She was raised with four brothers, two of whom have dedicated themselves to the ministry, and one sister, with Cris being the youngest of the six. Northeast Michigan is where Cris and her husband, Les, along with their loyal dog, Cookie, have chosen to live.

You can stay in touch with Cris on Facebook by following the username Cris Hoxie Author.

Printed in the USA
CPSIA information can be obtained
at www.ICGtesting.com
JSHW020018281223
54368JS00002B/57

9 798223 037286